Twayne's United States Authors Series

EDITOR OF THIS VOLUME

Kenneth Eble

University of Utah

American Political Writers: 1801–1973

AMERICAN POLITICAL WRITERS: 1801–1973

By EDWARD C. WILLIAMSON
Auburn University

TWAYNE PUBLISHERS
A DIVISION OF G.K. HALL & CO., BOSTON

Printed on permanent/durable acid-free paper and bound
in the United States of America

First Printing

Library of Congress Cataloging in Publication Data

Williamson, Edward C., 1916–
American political writers, 1801–1973

(Twayne's United States authors series ; TUSAS 394)
Bibliography: p. 171–82
Includes index.
1. Political Science—United States—History.
I. Title. II. Series.
JA84.U5W49   320.5′0973   81–1090
ISBN 0-8057-7327-4   AACR2

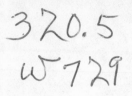

To Ethel, George, and Janet

Contents

About the Author

Edward C. Williamson, a professor of history at Auburn University, specializes in southern, political, and military history. He received his B.A. and M.A. degrees from the University of Florida and his Ph.D. from the University of Pennsylvania in 1954 with a dissertation on Florida politics after Reconstruction. He has published widely in the political, southern, and military fields. His book *Florida Politics in the Gilded Age 1877–1893* was published by the University Presses of Florida in 1976.

Professor Williamson has had an enriching career in both the academic and governmental fields. He has served as chief administrator for the Alabama colleges project, which provided expertise for the state's antipoverty programs. For several years he was chief editor for the United States Air Force Historical Division and also served as a combat historian in Korea for the Army. Professor Williamson has also held the position of associate editor for the *Textile History Review* and that of assistant editor for the *Florida Historical Quarterly*.

Professor Williamson has been a member of the Auburn University history department since 1957. He is Hollifield Professor of Southern History for 1981–83.

Preface

To achieve cohesion in a survey of American political writers in the time span from 1800 to 1973 is quite a challenge. This volume is the second part of a study of American political writers from 1588 to the present. The first volume, which ended in 1800, was written by Dr. Richard E. Amacher of Auburn University. In these books most major political writers who have been featured in separate volumes in the various Twayne series are treated *en passant*.

The beginning of the time span of this volume is marked by the first battle of the newly organized political parties, the Federalists and the Jeffersonian Republicans. The triumph of Thomas Jefferson over John Adams meant a changing of philosophy, a victory for the American liberalism of the day. A number of the better educated, more affluent, found themselves out of power. The laments of two of these disappointed conservatives, Fisher Ames and Joseph Dennie, reminds one of E. L. Godkin's later unsympathetic evaluation of the Populists and the more recent writing of William F. Buckley and Barry Goldwater.

Writers selected vary considerably in their frames of reference, their styles of writing, their persuasive arguments, and lastly, the audiences to whom they were projecting their ideas. They range all the way from utopian idealists to very practical realists. A conscientious effort has been made to present their viewpoints objectively and clearly. Topics emphasized before the Civil War include Jacksonian democracy, slavery, and the rise of the Republican party. An effort has been made to give both sides of issues.

After the Civil War, down to World War I, subjects include Reconstruction, the relationship between political thought and the rise of industrialism, Populism, and imperialism. I have particularly selected Populist writers whose reform-minded thinking was in a major way to influence the Progressive movement which occurred just prior to World War I. Greenwich Village provided a birthplace for twentieth-century American radicalism, and the New Left of the 1960s is a continuation of the thinking of the bohemians. Similarly to Populism, the New Deal caused a sharper differentiation between conservatism and liberalism. Issues selected after World War II, the debate between conservatives and liberals, the civil rights revolt, and the Vietnamese War provide both continuity and change in bringing this history of political writers to the present.

For my frame of reference I have primarily used original source material. For evaluation, as indicated in the text, I have, in addition to my own interpretations, utilized the fine works of Vernon Parrington, Henry Steele Commager, Merle Curti, Ralph Gabriel, Arthur Schlesinger, Jr., Roland Lora, Clinton Rossiter, and others.

In gathering source material I received particular assistance from Frances Honour, John Warner, Thomas Stratton, and other members of the staff of the Ralph Brown Draughton Library at Auburn University. I also appreciate the assistance given me by the staffs of the New York Public Library, the Library of Congress, and the office of Congressman Bill Nichols of Alabama.

I am grateful to Frances and Norman Perry, who proofread and commented on most of the chapters; to Ellen Ball who patiently typed the manuscript; and Joan Brokowsky, Gail Henderson, Flora Moss, and Sherri Sherwood of the Auburn History Department, who assisted me with final corrections. The Auburn University Research Grant-in-Aid Program generously gave financial assistance. And my wife Ruthie's patience and encouragement made this project a reality.

EDWARD C. WILLIAMSON

Auburn University

Chronology

1801   Inauguration of Thomas Jefferson.
1812–   War of 1812.
1815
1828   Andrew Jackson elected President.
1831   William Lloyd Garrison publishes first issue of the *Liberator*.
1834   Whig Party is formed.
1846   Mexican War
1850   Compromise of 1850.
1854   Republican party appears. Know-Nothing party is at its height.
1859   Abolitionist John Brown leads raid on Harpers Ferry, Virginia.
1860   Election of Lincoln.
1861–   Civil War.
1865
1877   End of Reconstruction.
1892   Strike at Carnegie Steel Mill at Homestead. Populist party makes strong bid in South and West.
1898   War with Spain.
1899–   War of Philippine Insurrection.
1902
1902   Muckrakers begin activities.
1914–   World War I.
1918
1920   Warren G. Harding elected president.
1929   Great Depression begins.
1933–   The New Deal.
1941
1939–   World War II.
1945
1945   Dropping of Atomic Bomb
1946   Beginning of Cold War
1950–   Korean Conflict
1953

1954 Brown v. *Board of Education of Topeka, Kansas.*
1964 Tonkin Gulf attack and resolution (Vietnamese Conflict).
1973 Withdrawal from Vietnam.

CHAPTER 1

Jeffersonian Republicanism

I *Introduction*

THE United States at the beginning of the nineteenth century was a sparsely populated newly independent republic. Although around ninety percent of the population was engaged in agriculture and other rural pursuits of livelihood, the commercial and business people of the few towns and small cities wielded considerable influence, far greater than their percentage of the population. The two most distinctive sections were the tidewater and the upcountry, a division that existed in all the tidewater states except Rhode Island and Delaware. New states Vermont, Tennessee, and Kentucky had the characteristics of the up-country. New England, composed of five states, was the most cohesive grouping.

The relatively few educated people held to two conflicting political philosophies. The Federalists, who were responsible for the Constitution, possessed a confidence in human reason which had been stimulated by Newton's scientific achievements. The Federalists also emphasized the rights of property by substituting "life, liberty and property" in the Constitution for the "life, liberty and the pursuit of happiness" of the Declaration of Independence. Influenced by Hobbesian concepts, they had a profound skepticism concerning democracy.[1] James Madison provided the philosophic pattern for the group combination responsible for the Constitution. For the new government George Washington was the unifying patriarch.[2] The strength of the Federalist party lay along the tidewater in New England, New York City, Philadelphia, and Charleston. Their principal leaders were John Adams and Alexander Hamilton.

Although limited to a minor role at the convention, partly because of his extreme nationalistic views, Hamilton—as the principal author of the *Federalist Papers*—was later to play an important part in the ratification of the Constitution. As secretary of the treasury of the first presidential administration, he was largely responsible for the somewhat less inclusive elitist group combination that dominated until 1800. The Federalist party included the *nouveau riche*, the shipping and mercantile interests, investors, speculators, as well as farmers and artisans tied economically to its policies. Nevertheless, neither Hamilton nor Adams was a clever political strategist, and the Federalists were never to become a cohesive political party that could bounce back from bitter defeat. Rather than Hamilton, Adams symbolized the high point of Federalist conservatism, "a love of the past and love of America combined with an awareness of sin, respect for order, property, and social classes."[3]

Until 1800 the party in power, the Federalists looked to England for both their philosophical base and for economic policies. Since their strength was in the tidewater, the Federalists faced the ocean rather than the backcountry. Their economic base was commerce. Their Bank of the United States was modeled on the Bank of England.

In the Washington administration the Anti-Federalists, the largely up-country opposition to the ratification of the Constitution, found their leader in Thomas Jefferson. By blending the ideas of the French philosophers with those of the frontier buckskins, Jefferson united the negative-oriented Anti-Federalists into a political party wth a positive philosophy. Neither party at this time was a mass-will type organization. The inner cores of both were composed of small and highly privileged elites. The Federalists were merchant princes, the Republicans planters and propertied precedent-rooted lawyers. Both would be strong on states' rights out of power, on nationalism in power.[4]

Although the victory of the Jeffersonian Republicans in 1800 was marred by the tie vote between Jefferson and his overly ambitious vice-presidential nominee, Aaron Burr, by the time of the inauguration Jefferson was firmly in control politically of both party and nation. His inaugural address was aimed at conciliating his old political foes: "But every difference of opinion, is not a difference of principle. We have called by different names brethren of the same principle. We are all republicans, we are all federalists."[5]

II   *John Taylor of Caroline*

As leader of the outs in both the 1790s and the election of 1800, Jefferson had favored states' rights over nationalism, country over town, and agrarianism over mercantilism. Here, he had a strong supporter in John Taylor, an aristocratic planter-lawyer of Caroline

County, Virginia. Although Taylor's principal writings were not to be published until several decades after the election of 1800, the Caroline political theorist had become a veritable storm center by the time of Jefferson's victory. The Virginia Federalist press labeled him "an anarchist, a friend to France, an enemy to America, and an office-seeker."[6]

Despite evident stylistic shortcomings, Taylor's writing was inclined to be verbose, repetitive, and disorganized, the planter-lawyer from Caroline summed up most adequately the agrarian argument against commercial capitalism, states' rights as opposed to federalism. His philosophy was that of a liberal agrarian. He "considered agriculture to be the guardian of liberty, as well as the mother of wealth."[7] In a strong appeal for the support of artisans and yeoman farmers, he attacked protective tariffs since "the device of protecting duties, under the pretext of encouraging manufactures . . . helps to rear up an aristocratical order, at the expense of the workers in earth, to unite with governments in oppressing every species of useful industry" (p. 20).

Taylor was not a libertarian or even an egalitarian, but a large slaveholder. He questioned the earlier antislavery position of Jefferson, explaining that Jefferson's *"Notes on Virginia* were written in the heat of a war for liberty; the human mind was made still hotter by the French revolution; and let those who were insensible of the mental fermentations and moral bubbles generated by these causes, censure Mr. Jefferson" (pp. 51–52). Nobly he would not do it. Paradoxically, Jacksonian democracy would follow more the position of Taylor than the earlier thesis of Jefferson insofar as slavery was concerned. Although Taylor called slavery a misfortune to agriculture, he considered the free blacks in the slave states a major threat to law and order. He felt that they should be either resettled in free states or established in a colony in Africa.[8]

The appeal of this aristocratic Virginian to the yeomanry was more of a commonality than a sharing of leadership. Naturally, the landed gentry were to be the leaders. Thus it should be recognized that Taylor's attacks on Federalist support of commerce and manufacturing were not intended to level society. Still it is paradoxical that Taylor should have been so strongly critical of John Adams's and Alexander Hamilton's views on aristocracy.[9] Despite his elitist tendencies, and largely because of his appeal to the yeomanry, Taylor would later be utilized as a bridge from Jeffersonian to Jacksonian democracy.[10] True, southern Republicans in general made no distinction between great planters and yeomen farmers. Taylor failed to see the irony of identification of people like himself with the French Physiocratic tradition and tillers of the soil. On slavery it is significant to note that before the passing of the thirteenth amendment not a single southern state freed its slaves.

Taylor's *An Inquiry into the Principles and Policy of the Government of the United States* took the philosophy of Adams and the authors of the Federalist Papers to task. He was particularly critical of any attempt to create an aristocracy since

among civilized people, no species of tyranny can exist, without the help of aristocracy. . . . [Further] aristocracy is no where agrarian. And wherever it has taken deep root in any form, an agricultural interest has ceased to be known or even spoken of, as having any influence in the government. . . . Whenever the lands of a country are so divided . . . so that the majority of the nation belong to the agrarian interest; no species of aristocracy, partaking in the least degree of a landed interest, can possibly be introduced.[11]

On political parties Taylor's views were unique. According to him

the United States exhibit four parties, the republican, monarchical, stock, and patronage. The two parties of principle, (Republican and monarchical), unsophisticated by the parties of separate interest, would discuss with moderation, and decide with integrity. . . . Aristocracy or separate interest . . . takes refuge under one and then under the other of our parties, because it is not yet able to stand alone. . . . It is thus that patronage transforms any party into an aristocracy of interest. . . . The patronage of the President of the United States, is aggravated by the temptation to employ it for his re-election. [p. 568]

The victory of Jeffersonian democracy in 1800 did not mean the demise of either conservative political criticism or writers who supported the Federalist party. The intellectual life of the young nation continued to remain in conservative hands. Conservative writers gained support and substance from England where Edmund Burke defended the authority of the past, of institutionalism, of property rights and the rule of the substantial class.[12] Incidentally, Jeffersonians and states' righters such as John Taylor followed a philosophy that was not entirely alien to that of Burke.

III   Fisher Ames

In the field of practical politics Fisher Ames of Dedham, Massachusetts, combined puritanical moral justification with Hamiltonian

merchant prince leadership. His elitist concept of the best government was the ideal Roman Republic which in reality never existed.[13]
Ames maintained that "to be the favorite of an ignorant multitude, a
man must descend to their level; he must desire what they desire,
and detest all they do not approve: he must yield to their prejudices,
and substitute them for principles. Instead of enlightening their
errors, he must adopt them. . . ."[14]

Ames identified the Puritan doctrine of the elect with the Yankee
doctrine of success.[15] He strongly opposed the effect of the French
Revolution on American politics. After Jefferson's election he feared
that with the demise of the Federalist party the nation would
collapse.[16]

In comparing the United States to the Roman Republic, Ames
asked:

Is the sovereign power to be contracted to a state centre? Is Virginia to be our
Rome? and are we to be her Latin or Italian allies. . . . The great state of
Virginia has fomented a licentious spirit among all her neighbours. Her
citizens imagine, that they are democrats, and their abstract theories are in
fact democratick; but their state policy is that of a genuine aristocracy or
oligarch. . . . For democratick license leads not to a monarchy regulated by
laws, but to the ferocious despotism of a chieftain, who owes his elevation to
arms and violence, and leans on his sword as the only prop of his dominion.
Such a conqueror, jealous and fond of nothing but his power, will care no
more for Virginia, though he may rise by Virginia, than Buonaparte does for
Corsica. Virginia will then find, that, like ancient Thebes, she has worked for
Philip, and forged her own fetters.[17]

Thus with Jefferson's election Ames saw only doom and despair.
The United States must sink into an anarchy out of which a military
despotism will arise similar to that of the French Revolution. To
prevent this catastrophe from wrecking New England, its citizenry
must remain a bastion of federalism.[18] Such a thesis would build up
sectionalism in New England in the same manner as did in the 1830s
John C. Calhoun's conclusions regarding his beloved South. Both
theses advocated a sectional veto of federal laws.

IV *Joseph Dennie*

Arriving in Philadelphia in 1799 to be secretary to Timothy Picker-
ing, secretary of state in Adams's cabinet, Joseph Dennie, a young
Boston lawyer, had reason to be bitter. Dennie had achieved a wide
reputation as a writer of Addisonian essays. His magazine, *The Port*

Folio, gained an extraordinary reputation. Interspersed among literary articles in *The Port Folio* were Dennie's pot shots at Jeffersonian style politics:

A democracy is scarcely tolerable at any period of national history. Its omens are always sinister, and its powers are unpropitious. With all the lights of experience, blazing before our eyes, it is impossible not to discern the futility of this form of government. It was weak and wicked in Athens. It was bad in Sparta, and worse in Rome. It has been tried in France, and has terminated in despotism. It was tried in England, and rejected with the utmost loathing and abhorrence. It is on trial here, and the issue will be civil war, desolation, and anarchy. No wise man but discerns its imperfections, no good man but shudders at its miseries, no honest man but proclaims its fraud, and no brave man but draws his sword against its force. The institution of a scheme of polity, so radically contemptible and vicious, is a memorable example of what the villainy of some men can devise, the folly of others receive, and both establish, in despite of reason, reflection, and sensation.[19]

In an essay on "Ingratitude of Republics" published in 1817 in *The Lay Preacher* after his death, Dennie again showed his elitist frame of reference as he complained of the lack of appreciation by his fellow Americans:

But judging from the practice of the world at the present time, one would think my text was grown obsolete and that its principle was not recognized. In the shambles there is always meat enough, but how little is bestowed upon workmen. Parasites, buffoons, fiddlers, equestrians, French philosophers, and speculators gormandize; but I see Merit, that excellent workman that needeth not to be ashamed, as lank and lean as my old tabby cat, who has had nothing to eat but church mice for a year.[20]

V *William Cobbett*

William Cobbett, English-born editor of Federalist newspapers, conducted a bitter pamphlet war on Republican editors Alexander D. Bache, William Duane, and Philip Freneau.[21] Cobbett resorted to personal attacks, particularly singling out President Jefferson. One such polemic Cobbett claimed, suspiciously, to be authored by a Jeffersonian Republican, long a member of Congress but now a minister to a foreign country. The vindictive anonymous author is most probably Cobbett.

In this attack the author asserted that Jefferson's ambitions have been more for literary fame than service to the country. Jefferson was also accused of timidity and vacillation. His friendship with Paine was an attack on Christianity. His elevation to the Presidency would result in a "whimsical, inconsistent, and feeble administration" which would subvert the Constitution in making the United States a satellite of France.[22]

VI *John Marshall*

Although after 1801 the Republicans controlled both the presidency and Congress, the Federalists continued for three decades to dominate the third branch—the judiciary. In the struggle that ensued some men, particularly the Jeffersonian Republicans, rejected the idea that the ratification of the Constitution had made the United States a federal union. But it was very much a federal union in the mind and decisions of Chief Justice John Marshall. States' righters received short shrift from Marshall; his biases were on the side of national unity, strong federal government, and judicial supremacy. He also supported the sanctity of private property and federal regulation of business. In his opinions and writings, the basic concepts of earlier natural law survived. His landmark judicial decisions unite the eighteenth-century doctrine of the sovereignty of the law with the new philosophy of capitalistic exploitation. Vernon Parrington has written that "the turbid waters of frontier leveling and states' rights democracy washed fiercely about him,"[23] never even wetting his shoes. He looked on democratic aspirations as calculated to destroy federal sovereignty. Even a fraudulent contract, involving both scandal and chicanery, was valid against state reform as in *Fletcher* v. *Peck*.[24]

Where the state, particularly one such as New Hampshire, dominated by Jeffersonian Republicans, attempted to usurp private property as in *Dartmouth* v. *Woodward*, Marshall stoutly defended the property holder. He held the sanctity of a contract in respect to property only since "the provision of the Constitution never has been understood to embrace other contracts than those which respect property or some object of value, and confer rights which may be asserted in a court of justice."[25]

In *McCulloch* v. *Maryland* (1819) Marshall enunciated a doctrine—later to be tested by the Civil War—to the effect that the government of the United States is supreme and that its laws take precedence to state constitutions and state laws.[26]

Jefferson regularly denounced the Marshall court for "driving us into consolidation." Marshall's great opinions were invariably aimed at striking down federal or state laws that either weakened the federal union or attacked the right of contract. Thus, as a jurist, while he built the federal government and protected the American capitalist, at the same time he limited public regulation of business.[27] Not until the New Deal would this be rectified.

VII   Mathew Carey

In the closing days of Jeffersonian democracy James Madison and James Monroe served as presidents. Madison's great moment in history was in the Constitutional Convention of 1787. He then excelled as the congressional leader of the outs and chief lieutenant of Jefferson. As chief executive he played the leading role in the involvement of the United States in the War of 1812, known derogatorily in New England as "Mr. Madison's War."

Against the unpopular background of the conflict in its darkest days Mathew Carey, a Philadelphia publisher, offered *The Olive Branch*.

I believe the country to be in imminent danger of a convulsion. . . . The nation is divided into two hostile parties, whose animosity towards each other is daily increased by inflammatory publications. Each charges the other with the guilt of having produced the present alarming state of affairs. . . . While a violent federalist believes all the evils of the present state of things have arisen from the guilt of the administration, nothing less will satisfy him than hurling Mr. Madison from the seat of government and sending him to Elba. While, on the other hand, a violent democrat persuades himself that all our evils have arisen from the difficulties and embarrassments constantly and steadily thrown in the way of the administration by the federalists, he is utterly averse to any compromise.—Each looks down upon the other with scorn and hatred, as the pharisee in the gospel, upon the publican. I have endeavoured to prove, and I believe I have fully proved, that each party has a heavy debt of error, and folly, and guilt, to answer for to their injured country, and to posterity. . . .[28]

Carey then attempted to define a middle ground between the Jeffersonian Republicans and Federalists. Concerned with the possibility of the dissolution of the union he poured oil on the troubled waters:

I plead not, fellow citizens, for democracy; I plead not for federalism. Their differences have sunk into utter insignificance. . . . I plead against jacobinism; I plead against faction; I plead against attempts to "overawe and controul the constituted authorities." I plead the cause of order; of government; of civil and religious liberty. I plead for the best constitution the world ever saw; I plead for your own honour as a party, which is in the utmost jeopardy. I plead for your bleeding country, which lies prostrate and defenceless, pierced with a thousand wounds. . . . I plead for your estates which are going to ruin. . . . Aid in extricating your country from danger. And then if you select calm and dispassionate, and moderate candidates for public office, there can be no doubt of your success. I am firmly persuaded that nothing but the intemperate and unholy violence of your leaders has prevented you from having that share of influence in the councils of the nation to which your wealth, your numbers, your talents, and your virtues, give you so fair a claim.

The constitution may be imperfect. Every thing partakes of human infirmity and human error. It has provided a proper mode of amendment. As soon as peace is restored, and the fermentation of public passions has subsided, let the real or supposed defects be brought fairly forward and submitted to the legislatures, or to a convention, as may be judged proper. [p. 342]

But, Carey maintained, "while the vessel of state is on rocks and quicksands, let us not madly spend the time, which ought to be devoted to secure her and our salvation, in the absurd and ill-timed attempt to amend, in other words to destroy, the charter party under which she sails" (p. 342).

He then tied in divine guidance with the preservation of the country. "May the Almighty Disposer of events inflame your hearts; enlighten your understanding; and direct you to the proper course to steer at this momentous crisis! And may he extend to our common country that gracious blessing which brought her safely through one revolution, without entailing on us the frightful curses inseparable from another!" [p. 342] After the war Mathew Carey turned from the theme of reconciliation to arguments for a protective system insofar as national industry was concerned. Following the Treaty of Ghent the businesses of new American manufacturers were seriously impaired by a flood of British goods. Carey painted a doleful picture of the American capitalist who

invests one hundred thousand dollars . . . engages hundreds of people in a useful and profitable manufacture; finally conquers all the various difficulties that new undertakings have to encounter; and brings his fabrics to market, in the hope of that reward to which industry, capital, and talent have so fair a claim. Alas! he has to meet not only the competition of his fellow citizens, but of all the manufacturing world. While he is excluded absolutely by prohibition, or virtually by prohibitory duties, from nearly all the markets in Europe, and indeed elsewhere; the East Indies, England, France, and Italy divide the home market with him, which is crowded with cargoes of similar articles, by the cupidity or the distresses, but as often by the stratagems, of foreign manufacturers, in order to overwhelm him, and secure the market ultimately to themselves. Their goods are sent to vendue, and sacrificed below prime cost in Europe. His cannot find a market, but at a sacrifice which ruins him. He implores relief from his unfeeling countrymen. But he implores in vain.[29]

Like Henry Clay, Carey made the cause of the manufacturer the cause of the nation. What he was advocating was an industrialized and self-sufficient United States independent of the rest of the world, with its manufacturers utilizing domestic raw materials and monopolizing the home market. He was particularly critical of the purchase of Indian cotton by American manufacturers, as well as the purchase by Americans of already manufactured cambrics and muslins in India and England. He claimed that because of Americans buying foreign imports, fifty textile manufacturers had recently left the United States. With this lack of protection

is it wonderful, that distress and embarrassment pervade the nation—that the enlivening sound of the spindle, the loom, and the hammer, has in many places almost ceased to be heard—that our merchants and traders are daily swept away by bankruptcy, one after another—that our banks are drained of their specie—that our cities exhibit an unvarying scene of gloom and despair—that confidence between man and man is almost extinct—that debts cannot in general be collected—that property cannot be sold but at enormous sacrifices—that capitalists have thus an opportunity of aggrandizing themselves at the expense of the middle class of society, to an incalculable extent—that money cannot be borrowed, but at an extravagant interest—in a word, that with advantages equal to any that Heaven has ever bestowed on any nation, we exhibit a state of things at which our enemies must rejoice—and our friends put on sackcloth and ashes?[30]

CHAPTER 2

Jacksonian Democracy

I *Democratic Party*

THE victory at New Orleans caused the War of 1812 to end with a surge of nationalism. This was reflected by a Congress that chartered the Second Bank of the United States, passed a protective tariff, and approved internal improvements. With the expiration of the presidential term of James Monroe, the last of the cocked hats, in an extremely close election in 1824—an election decided in the House of Representatives—John Quincy Adams emerged as victor. Then, just when it seemed that Jeffersonian democracy had ebbed sufficiently to allow the growth of a neo-Federalist movement, a grass roots revolt seized the national government from the hands of those who supported the political philosophies of Alexander Hamilton and John Adams. Jacksonian democracy had neither a Thomas Jefferson to lead it nor a John Taylor as its philosopher. Yet it was an all inclusive umbrella sheltering practically all those with rising expectations. In an antielitist, antiestablishment coalition Scotch-Irish yeomen farmers, westward moving, both proslavery and free soil, combined with the newly arrived Irish paddies of the eastern seaport towns. Fundamentalist agrarian folk joined with Catholic workingmen against the old entrenched moderate urban Protestant business and planter aristocracy.

Jacksonian democracy was a radical movement destined to break the power of the haves, level old barriers of exclusiveness, and open the way for government of a more popular character. Two great forces were behind it: first, frontier agrarianism in the West and South; second, industrialism and commercialism in the cities. Frontier life tended to produce self-reliance, independence, individuality, and a sense of equality. In piedmont town and country there was yet to be produced a leisure class, a highly polished society, and a historical and genealogical tradition. Newly arrived in the ghettoes of the coastal ports, the Irish paddy united with the descendants of those

23

old American blue-collar workers who with Sam Adams had thrown the tea into Boston harbor. The New York Irish quickly mastered the intricacies of Tammany politics. Their Achilles heel was a blind obsession against the British which made them most vulnerable to demagogues.

II   Orestes Brownson

Writing for the *Boston Quarterly Review* in 1839, New England intellectual Orestes Brownson defined political parties from the Jacksonian democratic viewpoint:

In all countries where there is life, where thought is active, and has scope to manifest itself in some degree, the community is divided into two parties more or less equal in numbers and strength. One party may be termed the Stationary Party, the party whose object is to retain things as they are, or to recall the order that is passing away; the other party may be termed the Movement Party, the party whose leading object is always to develop and improve the existing order, or to introduce a new, and, as it hopes, a better order. . . . These two parties have always existed here, and they showed themselves very distinctly in the Convention which framed the Federal Constitution. The party of Privilege, the aristocratic party, feeling themselves in the position to wield the power of the government, and of course to wield it in their own favor, asked for a strong government,—one capable of holding the people in awe, in check, in submission. The party of Equality, the democratic party, on the other hand, distrustful of governments, in consequence of having suffered from their abuses, demanded a weak government and a strong people; so that the few, by seizing its reins, should not be able to make the government trample on the rights and the interests of the many.[1]

In 1828 the supporters of John Quincy Adams and Henry Clay formed the National Republican party. In 1834 that party name changed when Clay and Daniel Webster, joined by the Anti-Masons, formed the Whig party. Whiggery, according to Brownson, was the "legitimate heir of the old Federal party, modified merely to meet the new questions which have come up" (129).

III   Whig Party

The Whig party became the party of the commercial interests, manufacturers, nativists, large planters, antislavery men, and Anti-Masons. It was divided between the cotton and conscience Whigs. To many of its members Jackson's election in 1828 and 1832

had been triumphs for King Mob, victories of rule by both the
unwashed and the ignorant. Even old Jeffersonians, including James
Madison and James Monroe, would not find white manhood suffrage
and sundry other elements of Jacksonian democracy to their liking.
The anonymously written *The Political Mirror of Review of
Jacksonism* attacked the old general, labeling his followers Tories,
and reviving the memory of the odious enemies of the Revolutionary
Whigs in an obvious attempt to steal the patriotic issue from the hero
of the War of 1812:

In a word, the doctrines of Jacksonism are party doctrines, and as such are to
be dreaded and combatted. We will exhibit a summary of them, and contrast
them with those professed by the Whigs. This exposition will show, that no
name was ever more misapplied, than that of Democratic Republicans,
which has been assumed by the Jackson party. Their true designation is *Tory*;
which has long characterized the party, which in free governments is opposed to representative democracy.[2]

The Whigs attempted to label the Democratic Republicans as
those, led by a dictatorial president, who were proponents of the
spoils system, free trade, and land speculation. They also criticized
Jackson's Indian policy as "might is right," despite treaties (pp.
310–15). Actually, Jacksonian democracy was a revival of Jeffersonian
Republicanism blended with the laissez faire doctrine of Adam Smith
and fresh influences, particularly of the frontier.[3] It meant bringing
to the fore a new generation of politicians with rising expectations,
including the strongly individualistic Sam Houston of Tennessee and
Texas, rugged Thomas Hart Benton of Tennessee and Missouri,
ex-Federalist James Buchanan of Pennsylvania, Martin Van Buren,
the little "Red Fox" of New York, and James K. Polk of Tennessee.
Since several prominent ex-Federalists joined the Jackson Democrats, Whig author Robert Mayo interpreted the movement as a
revival of Federalism. He also saw the Democratic party as made up
of "odds and ends of all parties, consisting of men of broken fortunes
and crooked principles, of easy consciences and adventurous
spirits. . . ."[4] He accused Jackson of involvement in the Burr plot
against Spanish America and then continuing this intrigue with Houston against Mexico.

General Jackson must have been actuated by some extraordinary secret
impulses connected with the inception and prosecution of the nefarious,
wicked, and piratical enterprise of General Houston against the integrity of

the Mexican dominions. A more searching analysis of the past, going back as far as Burr's conspiracy, will probably throw some further light upon this aspect of the matter in hand. There is . . . a series of connected passages in General Jackson's prime of life associated with that conspiracy. . . . . [p. 153]

IV   *William Leggett*

The *New York Evening Post*, ably edited by William Cullen Bryant and his associate editor and co-owner, William Leggett, strongly supported Jacksonian democracy. While still young, Bryant broke with the sectional and conservative beliefs of his native New England. He and Leggett were free traders and followers of Jeremy Bentham and English liberalism. They strongly advocated the laissez faire economic policy of the Jacksonians. Bryant also gave valuable and generous support to labor organizations in their struggle with inflexible employers and hostile courts. Workers, he maintained, had the right to unionize and to strike.[5]

With an early career which included being court-martialed out of the Navy because of insubordination, William Leggett did not bring the genteel tradition to the *Post*. As the philosopher of Gotham's Jacksonians, his style was lucid and picturesque. His invective was bloodcurdling, his use of irony excellent, and his editorials showed both good humor and gusto.[6] He did not look on Jackson with the same jaundiced view with which he earlier had appraised his naval commander. His view of Jackson was through rose colored glasses; he labeled the Whigs aristocrats:

The Aristocracy are exceedingly anxious to divert the attention of the people from the chief object of their warfare—the venerable and heroic old man who sits at the head of government. . . . General Jackson is hated by the aristocracy, and termed a usurper and a despot, a cut-throat and a villain. . . . The whole life of General Jackson has been one of absolute uncompromising devotion to his country. He never was afraid of responsibility when he was in jeopardy. He did not stand mooting nice points of political orthodoxy, or questioning whether he was right or wrong, when the ravager was on her shores, and the knife at her bosom. He is not the man who, when he sees his friend, his wife, or his country, suffering violence or injury, will stop to inquire who is to blame, before he flies to the rescue. He thinks of saving them first, and in his honest delight of having succeeded, forgets to ask the particulars of the quarrel. Is it any wonder that the honest, warm-hearted, clear-headed people of the United States love, and trust, and venerate this noble old man, whose redeemed pledges they see every day before them. . . .[7]

Actually, Jackson was one of the frontier aristocracy, a self-made man, true, but not a progressive politician. He never championed the cause of the people, but they were to champion his. In Tennessee his closest friends and advisors were old school conservatives, out of sympathy with frontier democracy.[8]

Leggett supported Jackson's attack on the banking system, particularly his advocacy of hard money. The New York editor felt that "the worst trash of bank rags" were palmed off on the workingmen. These were generally bought by employers in order to cheat their blue-collar employees. He suggested that short sentences, such as "Jackson and Hard Money!" be written on the back of every bank note by those who opposed "rag money."[9] Leggett strongly urged that

employers provide themselves with gold to pay their hands; and let the hands of those employers who continue in the practice, which has been too extensive, of procuring uncurrent money to pay them, take such measures to remedy the evil as are within their reach, and not inconsistent with prudence. The practice is wholly unjustifiable, and stands, in a moral point of view, on a footing not very different from that of clipping coins. . . . But though protected by the law, workmen may do much to rid themselves of the evils of this practise, and at the same time forward the great object of democracy—ultimate emancipation from the shackles of a destestable Bank tyranny. [p. 42]

V *Davy Crockett*

To attack Jackson—and more particularly his heir apparent Martin Van Buren—his enemies effectively used the name, and dubious talents, of Tennessee congressman Davy Crockett. Though his formal education was limited to six months schooling, Crockett was a master at ridicule and humor, in addition to having been an excellent hunter and Indian scout. One of the few to have served under the old general and not supported him politically, Crockett explained:

I like Genral [sic] Jackson as a general; but he is too passionate and arbitrary for the rule of a free people; and therefore his opinions, in civil matters, should be received with many grains of allowance. He suffers himself to be imposed upon by understrappers—men who can't look an honest man in the face. . . . [T]he deep interest he takes in Van Buren's election is an *unnatural one*, excited by the worst of means, in favour of a man who has no other regard for him (and so manifested the fact by going over to his support when he could do not better). . . . He has been duped into an unnatural alliance.[10]

In an effort to defeat Van Buren's presidential bid in 1836 Crockett had been brought to New York City the previous year. Turned Whig publicist he disparaged Van Buren's followers:

. . . I asked Colonel Webb to go with me to the "Five-points," a noted place near the centre of the city. This is the place where Van Buren's warriors came from during the election, when the wild Irish, with their clubs and bludgeons, knocked down every one they could find that would not huzza for Jackson. . . . Black and white, white and black, all hug-em-snug together, happy as lords and ladies, sitting sometimes round in a ring, with a jug of liquor between them: and I do think I saw more drunk folks, men and women, that day, than I ever saw before. This is part of what is called by the Regency the "glorious sixth ward"—the regular Van Buren ground-floor I thought I would rather rique [sic] myself in an Indian fight than venture among these creatures after night.[11]

Crockett contended that the Whigs and himself were the true patriots and he "thanked God for giving me fortitude enough to stand firm, and support the constitution and the laws" (42). Jackson supporters he termed Tories who should be sent up and over Salt river (p. 46). His old general he compared to the British king at the time of the Revolution: "I consider we are returning to the old days of King George the Third as fast as possible; we then had the government of one man, and agreeable to my understanding, we have arrived nearly to the same point again, in these glorious days of retrenchment and reform" (p. 129). Defeated by Jackson forces in Tennessee, Crockett moved to Texas, where in his autobiography he gave some advice to aspiring young politicians. He suggested that they attend all public meetings, chairing if possible, join the militia as officers, be elected to the legislature, and attack their state's constitution. Further,

when the day of election approaches, visit your constituents far and wide. Treat liberally, and drink freely. . . . True, you may be called a drunken dog by some of the clean shirt and silk stocking gentry, but the real rough necks will style you a jovial fellow—their votes are certain, and frequently count double. Do all you can to appear to advantage in the eyes of the women. That's easily done—you have but to kiss and slabber [slobber over] their children, wipe their noses, and pat them on the head; this cannot fail to please their mothers. . . . Promise all that is asked . . . and more if you can think of any thing. Offer to build a bridge or a church, to divide a county, create a batch of new offices, make a turnpike, or any thing they like. Promises cost nothing, therefore deny nobody who has a vote or sufficient influence . . . and when once elected, why a fig for the dirty children, the promises, the bridges, the churches, the taxes, the offices, and the subscriptions, for it is absolutely necessary to forget all these before you can become a thorough-going politician, and a patriot of the first water.[12]

VI   *Benjamin Fanevil Hunt and Hugh A. Garland*

Other southerners came north with views opposite to those of Crockett. There were many such strong political ties between workingmen of the city and the southern farmer-planters. Those whom Crockett looked upon as rabble were cultivated by southern aristocrats Colonel Benjamin Fanevil Hunt of Charleston and Hugh A. Garland of Virginia. In 1840 Hunt, speaking in New York, attacked the Whig party:

I am your fellow citizen, equally interested with you in the great and eventful contest which now agitates this whole country. . . . The antagonist party contended for a general consolidated government, similar to the monarchies of Europe, and the perfect subordination of the states to the federal head. . . . [T]ime has now arrived . . . to decide . . . whether the struggles of the revolution are to secure to us and our posterity the blessings of a democracy, or are to end at last in the subserviency of the laboring and industrious classes to a moneyed aristocracy, whose roots reach, in all probability, beyond the Atlantic.[13]

Hunt emphasized the common interests of the urban workingmen and the southern farmers, since "with the cotton of the south, the planter can't eat it, nor he can't drink it, nor he can't smoke it. He has to sell the whole of it; and if prices fall. . . . [H]e has to buy all that he wants for his own use out of the diminished sum which his produce yields him."[14]

The same year Hugh A. Garland, a Jackson Democrat from Virginia, reinforced for the New Yorkers the logic of Hunt concerning the common interests of planters, yeoman farmers, and workingmen against the creditor merchant-banker Whigs. Garland's special target was the supporters of the defunct Bank of the United States, since that financial institution

had organized a consolidated, well disciplined band of men, thoroughly imbued with aristocratic notions of the nobility of money, the degradation of labor, and was boldly and openly aspiring to absolute legislative as well as commercial control. . . . But the spirit of freedom still hovered over the land. . . . On the Fourth of July, 1832, the hero of the iron nerve, pronounced the sovereign will of the people, and proclaimed to the world, that the bastile of tyranny and usurpation should be leveled with the earth; the mother of Jacobins should no longer hold a place among the living.[15]

VII   *T. R. Hazard*

Whigs did not totally desert the fight for workingman votes. Whig writer, T. R. Hazard of Newport, who claimed to be a laboring man, warned that

before the glowing blessings of the specie system about to be introduced, have begun to produce this rich harvest of prosperity, and thereby blinded your eyes to the few redeeming traits of our hitherto "false system" of tariff, credit, railroads, canals, "bank and rags" . . . perhaps you may then discover that Henry Clay, and the host of bustling, active, business-working men, who acted in concert to plan and perfect this "false system" of credit and home labor protection, had occasional glimmerings of common sense. . . .[16]

VIII   *Summary*

The writers supporting Jacksonian democracy generally abandoned the affectations of those of the Jeffersonian era, replacing them with hard-hitting, less pedantic arguments that attacked privilege and aristocracy, glorified the common man, and created from a war hero the tribune of the people. As a pseudo-Jacksonian Davy Crockett used homespun humor to defend the Whig position, which held that Jackson was prototype of George III. Similar to the Federalists, Hazard attempted to make the full dinner pail a prime reason for a worker to become a Whig and a follower of Henry Clay.

CHAPTER 3

Proslavery Thought

I Introduction

IN the settlement of the original thirteen colonies during the mid-seventeenth century the institution of slavery replaced the system of indenture. Particularly in the Chesapeake Bay tobacco plantations the African black supplanted the European bonded servant. The slave trade involved mainly two colonial business classes: the New England ship owners and the southern planters. Although the bulk of the slaves labored in the six planter colonies south of the Mason and Dixon Line, slavery existed in all thirteen colonies.

Results of the liberal thinking engendered by the American Revolution included the elimination of slavery in the seven northern nonplantation states and a flourishing antislavery movement in the South. By the end of the eighteenth century, scorched by the pens of such enlightened men as Thomas Jefferson and starved by the decline of tobacco and indigo, slavery appeared a dying institution, an anachronism that would go the way of the quitrent, mercantilism, and primogeniture. A possible, but not very practical solution, was offered by the American Colonization Society, which, beginning in 1817, proposed emancipating slaves and returning them to Africa. Since blacks in the South presented not only a problem in numbers but also in capital, few slaveholders seemed willing to take a laissez faire free market position toward labor. Wait and see best describes their attitude.

Because slavery was not a thriving institution at the time of the Constitutional Convention and was directly contrary to the concepts proclaimed by the Declaration of Independence, why was this awesome problem not solved then and there? Only two states, South Carolina and Georgia, strongly supported its continuance. The answer is in the conservatism of the American cultural pattern. The Constitutional Convention was a meeting of conservatives who were not there to rock the boat but to make it more stable. Though in 1787 almost all proslavery people were in agreement that the institution was a necessary evil, no serious consideration was given its abolition. The organized church, with the exception of the Quakers, showed no inclination to advocate its end. It is most significant that after the momentum of Revolutionary War liberalism not a single state freed its slaves before the Civil War. Indeed, emancipation was a far more difficult task in the 1850s than it had been in the 1790s. The proslavery forces were far more powerful in 1860 than they had been in 1787.

II　*Slavery Becomes a Positive Good*

Just as the Yankee slave traders, among others, kept the southern plantations supplied in the colonial period, a Yankee inventor revitalized the institution with the invention of the cotton gin in 1793. As cotton planters moved westward following the Battle of Horseshoe Bend they were unimpeded in the lush lower south lands of Mississippi and Alabama. But insofar as border territory Missouri in 1820 was concerned, stiff northern opposition to the extension of slavery caused sharp debate. The aged but still sharp Jefferson exclaimed: "This momentous question, like a fire bell in the night, awakened and filled me with terror. I considered it at once the knell of the Union."[1] In Congress a cross section of northerners irritated their southern colleagues by asserting that slavery was wrong according to the dictates of humanity, the teachings of the Scripture, and the principles of democracy.

Still, a few years later, in 1827, out of a total of 130 antislavery societies, all moderate, 106 existed in slave states. The Quakers were most active in the North Carolina Manumission Society with forty-five branches. Unfortunately, this organization went into a decline in 1828.[2] The Nat Turner revolt in August 1831 precipitated a debate in the Virginia legislature the following January during which various legislators denounced slavery as a social canker, an economic blight, and a moral evil, and demanded a program of gradual emancipation. Unfortunately, the reformers were defeated. In the decade that followed the South came to support a proslavery no-reform consensus. By 1837 not a single antislavery society remained active in the South. An intellectual climate that earlier had made possible a healthy degree of conflict between Federalists and Republicans and had served to stimulate ideas and encourage development no longer existed. One either defended the southern way of life or moved elsewhere. Within this narrow framework, though, Jacksonian democracy struggled with Whiggery. Ambivalence is ever the American way of life.

In the change of climate John C. Calhoun of South Carolina emerged as the political leader of the proslavery forces. Speaking in the senate in February 1837, Calhoun argued that the union and abolition could not co-exist. To attempt to force the South to relinquish slavery would result in war. Insofar as slavery was concerned Calhoun asserted that "the relation now existing in the slaveholding states between the two is, instead of an evil, a good—a positive good."[3]

III   *Thomas Roderick Dew*

Although the North was not united in its opposition to slavery, the conflict was now between regions. In the South abolitionist literature from the North served to bolster proslavery unity, not exactly its intended purpose. Slavery's protagonists came from the mainstream of the southern middle class. Defense of slavery became synonymous with defense of one's way of life. Along with politicians, academicians, and agrarian utopians all argued the same theme. Although his predecessors on the William and Mary faculty had been antislavery, Thomas Roderick Dew maintained that the inequality of man was fundamental to all social organization. His views had wide influence in the South.[4] His theme was racial inferiority. In *An Essay on Slavery* he reasoned that

in looking to the texture of the population of our country, there is nothing so well calculated to arrest the attention of the observer, as the existence of negro slavery throughout a large portion of the confederacy. A race of people differing from us in color and in habits, and vastly inferior in the scale of civilization, have been increasing and spreading, growing with our growth, and strengthening with our strength, until they have become intertwined with every fibre of society. Go through our southern country, and every where you see the negro slave by the side of the white man; you find him alike in the mansion of the rich, the cabin of the poor, the workshop of the mechanic, and the field of the planter. . . . Can these two distinct races of people, now living together as master and servant, be ever separated? Can the black be sent back to his African home, or will the day ever arrive when he can be liberated from his thraldom, and mount upwards in the scale of civilization and rights, to an equality with the white? This is a question of truly momentous character; it involves the whole frame work of society, contemplates a separation of its elements, or a radical change in their relation, and requires for its adequate investigation the most complete and profound knowledge of the nature and sources of national wealth and political aggrandizement. . . .[5]

The power of reasoning ended with Dew's assertion that "every plan of emancipation and deportation is *totally* impracticable." Further, he took issue with the propriety of making abolition a public issue in "consequence of the injurious effects which might be produced on the slave population." Dew's justification of slavery involved old chestnuts: the Bible, history, the laws of war, and the rights of property (pp. 3–8, 34–56).

IV *William Harper*

Born in the West Indies, of Scotch-Irish background, William Harper graduated from South Carolina College as its first student in 1805. Formerly a nationalist, by 1830 he had become a convert to nullification.[6] His *Memoir on Slavery* (1837) maintained that those who had superior faculties and knowledge should control those who were inferior. He also claimed that slavery both emphasized the benefits and retarded the evils of civilization.[7] At the same time, he defended corporal punishment:

If the state of slavery is to exist at all, the master must have, and ought to have, such power of punishment as will compel them to perform the duties of their station. Has the master any temptation to go beyond this? If he inflicts on him such punishment as will permanently impair his strength, he inflicts a loss on himself. . . . It is true that the slave is driven to labor by stripes; and if the object of punishment be to produce obedience or reformation, with the least permanent injury, it is the best method of punishment. . . . Such punishment would be degrading to a freeman . . . it is not degrading to a slave. . . [pp. 30, 34].

Even to the argument that a slave was deprived of intellectual, moral, and religious improvement, Harper had an answer. To this he admitted, but God had not intended all human beings to "be highly cultivated, morally and intellectually." Instead, there was to "be general mediocrity." Nevertheless, "by the existence of Slavery, exempting so large a portion of our citizens from the necessity of bodily labor, that we have a greater proportion than any other people, who have leisure for intellectual pursuits, and the means of attaining a liberal education" (p. 35).

A student of ancient history, Harper claimed that the loss of domestic slavery was a major cause for the decline of both Rome and Greece (p. 70). He blamed slave unrest in the South largely on abolitionist agitation, since the blacks there were "the happiest three millions of human beings on whom the sun shines" (p. 133). Into their Eden has come Satan in the guise of the abolitionist. For the past fifty years slaves have been admonished by abolitionists that they were "victims of the most grinding and cruel injustice and oppression" (p. 76). Further, in a thousand channels they were able to propagandize the blacks and constantly exhorted them to insurrection. Masters were described as criminals, tyrants, and robbers. Since in the not so distant past slavery in the South was viewed as "a great evil, unjust and indefensible in principle," southerners in some measure had pleaded guilty (pp. 76–78). Harper even justified slavery from the viewpoint of national defense, claiming that under it the able-bodied free white males would constitute a large, readily available military force able to take the field without disturbing the labor supply (p. 79).

Harper agreed with the abolitionists that emancipation, if decided upon, should be immediate and total. The most obvious result of this would be the end of King Cotton because the former plantation laborers would migrate elsewhere to become propertyholders. On the plantations, now dependent upon free labor, a strike could cause the destruction of the entire crop. Then, too, the freeing of the slaves would cut down on the cotton raised, end the exporting of cotton, and eliminate from two-thirds to three-fourths of American foreign commerce (pp. 86–87). Of the blacks

We know that nothing but the coercion of Slavery can overcome their propensity to indolence, and that not one in ten would be an efficient laborer. . . . Half our population would at once be paupers. Let an inhabitant of New-York or Philadelphia conceive of the situation of their respective States, if one-half of their population consisted of free negroes. . . . Released from the vigilant superintendence which now restrains them, they would infallibly be led from petty to greater crimes, until all life and property would be rendered insecure. [p. 89]

Their acquisition of voting rights was unthinkable, since "if the free blacks were given the franchise, unprincipled demagogues would use them. If they attained political ascendancy, there would be mass migration from the United States" (p. 90).

V *James H. Hammond*

Also contained in *The Pro-Slavery Argument* were letters from
Governor James H. Hammond of South Carolina to Thomas
Clarkson, president of the British Anti-Slavery Society, answering a
circular letter to professing Christians in northern states. Son of a
northerner who had settled in the Carolina back country, Hammond,
also a graduate of South Carolina College, had been a newspaper
writer, lawyer and planter.[8] Similar to Dew and Harper he maintained that slavery not only was "an inexorable necessity for the
present, but a moral and humane institution, productive of the
greatest political and social advantages. . . ."[9] Further, he asserted
that slavery was "not only not a sin, but especially commanded by
God through Moses, and approved by Christ through his apostles" (p.
108).

Encouraged by their English counterparts, the American
abolitionists were "incessantly threatening to dissolve the Union" (p.
109). Thus he placed slavery on the side of God and country. The
South was a law abiding land of purity free of radicalism. It was to its
credit

that few of the remarkable religious *Isms* of the present day have taken root
among us. We have been so irreverent as to laugh at Mormonism and
Millerism, which have created such commotions farther North; and modern
prophets have no honor in our country. Shakers, Rappists, Dunkers,
Socialists, Fourrierists and the like, keep themselves afar off. Even Puseyism
has not yet moved us. You may attribute this to our domestic Slavery if you
choose. I believe you would do so justly. [p. 117]

Hammond admitted that activities of abolitionists had caused
slaveholders to rely more and more on the power of fear. Efforts to
attach slaves to them through affection and pride had to be curtailed.
The system of slavery was not in a state of decay. Southerners were
determined to remain masters. However, if the slaves were freed that
would end cotton culture (pp. 126–27, 147).

VI *William Gilmore Simms*

William Gilmore Simms, one of the few outstanding Southern
writers of the antebellum era, defended with considerable passion
slavery from the attacks of Harriet Martineau, an English

abolitionist. Martineau, with a keenly observant eye, wrote critically of her travels through the South. Simms asserted that when he first defended slavery in 1837

little had been said in defence of African Slavery in America. Prescription was against it everywhere. All our maxims, our declamation, the pet phrases, equally of philanthropy and of demagogueism, were designed to render it odious and criminal; and, in the defence usually offered, on the part of those who maintained it, it was generally admitted that a wrong had been done, and that a social evil did exist, which expediency alone denied that we should seek to repair, or put away from us.[10]

Simms modestly asserted that he had been among the first to take the high ground that no wrong had been done the black in making him a slave. Instead it had been a great good and blessing. The institution of slavery existed under the "immediate sanction of Heaven" (p. 178). Reviewing its history Simms maintained that slavery had not been abolished in the North. "It simply died out, when it ceased to be profitable." The New England states chiefly excelled in slave trading, stealing the blacks from Africa, keeping only a few. It was from the southern states that the first call came to end the international slave trade. Even now, New Englanders were still in the slave trade which was piracy (pp. 200–201). "Emancipation and the pettings of philanthropy" lifted the coarse and uneducated black

into a condition to which his intellect did not entitle him, and to which his manners were unequal;—he became presumptuous accordingly, and consequently offensive;—and the whites, who could have tolerated him in his proper and inferior condition, were naturally outraged by the impudence of the creature when lifted out of place. There is no doubt that he is an object of dislike and hatred in the Northern cities, and with good reason. . . . The blacks . . . will not labor at all if they can escape it. They will do jobs, do light chores, brush boots, go on errands, sweep, tinker, and thieve. . . . He must be always despicable in any community which leaves him at liberty, and where he shrinks from grappling with the higher toils and purposes which alone can dignify the possession of freedom.

The case is far otherwise where Negro Slavery exists. In the South, the negro is not an object of dislike or hatred. There, he never offends by obtrusiveness; he occupies his true position, and, while he fills it modestly, he is regarded with favor, nay, respect and love, and is treated with kindness and affection. [pp. 213–14]

VII   *William J. Grayson*

During this period, William J. Grayson, former congressman and collector of customs at Charleston, South Carolina, wrote a poem, *The Hireling and the Slave*. A unionist and a moderate among firebrands, Grayson held that the status of the northern worker and the slave was identical. Slavery was preferable since the abolitionists did nothing for slaves whereas the planters had changed them from savages to civilized people.[11]

How small the choice, from cradle to the grave,
Between the lot of hireling, help, or slave!
To each alike applies the stern decree
That man shall labor; whether bond or free
For all that toil, the recompense we claim-
Food, fire, a home and clothing-is the same.
. . . .

  And yet the life, so unassailed by care,
So blessed with moderate work, with ample fare,
With all the good the starving pauper needs,
The happier slave on each plantation leads;
Safe from harassing doubts and annual fears,
He dreads no famine in unfruitful years;
If harvests fail from inauspicious skies,
The master's providence his food supplies;
No paupers perish here for want of bread,
Or lingering live, by foreign bounty fed;
No exiled trains of homeless peasants go,
In distant climes, to tell their tales of woe. . . .[12]

VIII   *George Fitzhugh*

Around 1856 Virginia attorney George Fitzhugh on a visit north, at the home of his abolitionist relative Gerrit Smith, met Harriet Beecher Stowe. Returning south a stouter defender of slavery, Fitzhugh followed Grayson with *Cannibals All! or Slaves without Masters*, a book which contrasted the security of the slave with the uncertainty of the northern workingman.[13]

The negro slaves of the South are the happiest, and, in some sense, the freest people in the world. The children and the aged and infirm work not at all, and yet have all the comforts and necessaries of life provided for them. They enjoy liberty, because they are oppressed neither by care nor labor. The women do little hard work, and are protected from the despotism of their husbands by their masters. The negro men and stout boys work, on the average, in good weather, not more than nine hours a day. The balance of their time is spent in perfect abandon.[14]

Just as Fitzhugh is an expert on plantation labor so also is he a self-appointed expert on the free labor system. The capitalistic society, functioning according to the laissez faire doctrines of Adam Smith, was a total failure. Fitzhugh makes a sharp distinction between plantation capitalism and the industrial variety. The industrial variety deserved the denunciation of the utopian socialists. In *sharp* contrast to the slaves who

with their faces upturned to the sun . . . can sleep at any hour. . . . We do not know whether free laborers ever sleep. They are fools to do so; for, whilst they sleep, the wily and watchful capitalist is devising means to ensnare and exploitate them. The free laborer must work or starve. He is more of a slave than the negro, because he works longer and harder for less allowance than the slave, and has no holiday, because the cares of life with him begin when its labors end. He has no liberty, and not a single right. [p. 30]

Thus the businessman who hires free laborers is a schemer and a Scrooge. The businessman who purchased slaves is a humanitarian. Fitzhugh warned that as modern civilization advanced, slavery became more necessary for the free worker as capital was accumulated by a few people. In such a situation as a free competitive society Christian morality would find little practical foothold. He labeled abolitionists as dangerous radicals who supported Negro's rights, women's rights, free love, anarchy, and socialism (pp. 46–47, 312).

IX *Summary*

Many northern businessmen preferred peace over an abolitionist war against the institution of slavery. Thus it is not surprising that certain northern political writers gave support to the southern way of life.[15]

There can be no reasonable doubt that southern support of the institution of slavery, such support reinforced by friendly Yankees, was a prime cause of the Civil War. Did slaveholders have a feeling of guilt? Could they see that other than "sterile rhetoric" and "special pleading" there was not a strong defense of the peculiar institution? Could they see that the civilized world was against them? The answer must be yes. Still, the slaveholders reassured each other that their consciences were clear and that the slaves were "the happiest people in the world, and do not wish to be placed in any other condition."[16]

American political writing has often blended the theoretical with the practical. The proslavery authors, including their great political leader, John C. Calhoun, illustrate this point well. In defense of a primarily economic institution—which slavery was—their arguments draw support from the Bible, Roman law, and the myth that slaves imported from Africa were savages. It is not overly critical to say that no proslavery writer attempts to give a realistic picture of bondage. They were propagandists insofar as their descriptions of the "peculiar" institution were concerned.

CHAPTER 4

Antislavery Thought

I Introduction

IN the Revolutionary period the antislavery movement included
first line leadership, including Benjamin Franklin, Thomas Jefferson, Alexander Hamilton, and John Jay. The seven northern states in
the era following the war freed their slaves, making the Mason-Dixon
line the most critical boundary in United States history. Later, during
the second administration of Thomas Jefferson, the African slave
trade was terminated. The political balance between slave and free
states was achieved by the admission of Tennessee to the Union in
1796 and continued by the Missouri Compromise. With the rise of
King Cotton after the War of 1812 the antislavery movement in the
South collapsed, particularly after the defeat of antislavery forces in
Virginia's House of Delegates in the debates of 1831–1832.

II William Lloyd Garrison

The leadership of the antislavery forces, largely a radical grouping
isolated from seats of political and economic power, centered on
William Lloyd Garrison, a hitherto obscure itinerant printer who in
1828 set up shop in Boston. He partially selected Boston because of
the apathy toward slavery in the North:

During my recent tour for the purpose of exciting the minds of the people
. . . on the subject of slavery, every place I visited gave fresh evidence of the
fact, that a greater revolution in public sentiment was to be effected in the
free states—and particularly in New England—than at the South. I found
contempt more bitter, opposition more active, detraction more relentless,
prejudice more stubborn, and apathy more frozen than among slave owners
themselves.[1]

On 1 January 1831 he printed the first issue of *The Liberator*, asserting

to the 'self evident truth' maintained in the American Declaration of Independence, that all men are created equal, and endowed by their Creator with certain inalienable rights—among which are life, liberty, and the pursuit of happiness, I shall strenuously contend for the immediate enfranchisement of our slave population.

Deliberately, he took an extreme position, calling for the immediate abolition of slavery. Resentment toward abolitionism in the North, and toward Garrison in particular, was so strong that in 1835 he was dragged through the streets of Boston by a mob and almost killed. His appeal for abolition was free of any taint of moderation.

I am aware, that many object to the severity of my language; but is there not cause for severity. I *will be* as harsh as truth, and as uncompromising as justice . . . I do not wish to think, or speak, or write with moderation. No! No! Tell a man whose house is on fire, to give a moderate alarm; tell him to moderately rescue his wife from the hands of the ravisher; tell the mother to gradually extricate her babe from the fire into which it has fallen;—but urge me not to use moderation in a cause like the present. I am in earnest—I will not equivocate—I will not excuse—I will not retreat a single inch—AND I WILL BE HEARD.[2]

III   *Garrison's Feud with James G. Birney*

The political abolitionists were principally westerners led by Kentuckian James G. Birney, who in 1840 and 1844 with the Liberty party had no more success nationally than Harold Stassen in recent years. One year prior to the first campaign of the abortive antislavery third party, Birney engaged in a controversy with William Lloyd Garrison on the issue of political activism. Birney maintained that "association for accomplishing objects to which the consent of the majority is necessary, is called for, only on the ground, that the sentiment of the majority as to the particular object, differs from that of the minority who associate."[3] Thus it was the object of the minority to change the opinion of that majority.

Therefore, the political organization of antislavery people was the best route for winning over public opinion. A year after the American Anti-Slavery Society came into existence, Birney recalled that Garrison not only voted for a professed abolitionist but encouraged others to do so. Birney also pointed out that the constitutions of the various

antislavery state societies contained no prohibitions forbidding political action. He labeled Garrison and his followers "No-Government
abolitionists." These did not vote, yet petitioned Congress, an inconsistent position (p. 5). Since the constitution of the American Anti-
Slavery Society required its members to vote, Birney saw

no good reason why the No-Government party should *wish* to remain in the
Anti-Slavery Association, seeing it must be productive of endless
dissentions;—especially, when, by withdrawing and forming on a platform of
their own, they could conduct their enterprise vigorously and harmoniously,
and permit the abolitionists, who are the advocates of the elective franchise,
to do the same with theirs. . . . It is in vain to think of succeeding in
emancipation without the co-operation of the great mass of the intelligent
mind of the nation. This can be attracted, only by the reasonableness, the
religion, of our enterprise. To multiply causes of repulsion is but to drive it
from us, and ensure our own defeat—to consign the slave to perdurable
chains—our country to imperishable disgrace. [pp. 12–13]

In reply Garrison called Birney's views extraordinary and a bold
attack upon abolitionists of pacifist leaning. This attack opened up the
whole question of nonresistance. Garrison objected strongly to being
called a No-Government man. He much preferred the term nonresis-
tant (pp. 16, 34).

He might as honestly style us a [*sic*] banditti. Mr. Birney is called, by the
pro-slavery party, "a fanatic," "a madman," and "an incendiary." . . . Why,
then, is he so unjust as to fasten upon us a name which was coined in the mint
of slander. . . . We deny the accusation. We religiously hold to
government—a strong, a righteous, a perfect government—a government
which is indestructible, which is of heaven, not of men, which tolerates no
evil, which is administered by an infallible Judge, an impartial Lawgiver, the
King of kings, and Lord of lords. [p. 16]

Garrison advocated the abolition of the ballot box and a miraculous
reform of every legislative assembly. He argued that it was the duty of
every voter to be an abolitionist. When this happened slavery could
be abolished.

IV *William Goodell*

Supporting Birney's position, antislavery moderate William
Goodell thought it possible to eliminate slavery constitutionally.
Born in upstate New York and self-educated, Goodell was also a

temperance man and a women suffrage reformer.[4] He saw both good and bad emerging from several schisms among the abolitionists. A favorable consequence coming from division was the reaching of more people. For example, the Liberty party favored political abolitionism.[5] Church reformers favored missionary abolitionism. As a result the two major political parties and the churches adopted the issue:

> Politicians were careful to supply a Whig and a Democratic abolitionism. No man knew where to go to escape the infection. He could not elude it in the religious sect, nor in the political party. If he cried out against abolitionism as "bigotry, priestcraft, and Puritanism," behold! there was the most rampant abolitionism, at his elbow, railing lustily against "bigotry, priestcraft, Puritanism and pro slaveryism"—placing them all in a row. If one sought, in view of this, to disparage abolitionism as heretical and infidel, behold! the gathering of an antislavery conference and prayer meeting met his vision. . . . The simpleton who had but just learned from his political editor to curse the abolitionists, was puzzled to find the same editor, or perhaps his Congressional candidate, professing to be as good an abolitionist as anybody. [p. 561]

Goodell maintained that earnest and acrimonious debates among the abolitionists had displaced the controversy between abolitionists and proslavery people. Further, these debates had broadened the coverage of the abolitionists. The issue was now "*not* whether slavery *ought* to be abolished nor *when* it should be—but, by what methods and motives should the" community be involved (p. 561).

V *William Ellery Channing*

Massachusetts pacifist William Ellery Channing represented a middle ground in the antislavery movement. Harvard educated, Channing had served as a tutor in the Richmond home of David Meade Randolph. In his discussions on slavery he addressed the conscience of the South rather than that of New England.[6] The first question concerning slavery was "not what is profitable, but what is Right. All prosperity not founded on right was built on sand."[7]

With a background of opposition to the War of 1812, Channing was very much an idealistic opponent of violence.[8] He gently supported the antislavery movement but warred against extremism and emotionalism. The agitation of the abolitionists, he thought, had "made converts of a few individuals, but alienated multitudes":[9] "A community can suffer no greater calamity than the loss of its principles. Lofty and pure sentiment is the life and hope of a people. . . . [T]o espouse a good cause is not enough. . . . Even sympathy with the injured and oppressed may do harm, by being partial, exclusive, and bitterly indignant" (pp. 9–10).

Channing was most critical of "the sending of pamphlets by the Abolitionists into the Slave-holding States" (p. 125). Rather than converting slaveholders, the activities of the abolitionists had been a prime cause of southerners defending slavery "in the spirit of the dark ages, and in defiance of the moral convictions and feelings of the Christian and civilized world" (p. 133). Northern states had duties to perform toward the South. Among these was the prevention of insurrection plots, "to frown on passionate appeals to the ignorant, and on indiscriminate and inflammatory vituperation of the slaveholder" (p. 139). On the other hand, free states should "use every virtuous influence for the abolition of slavery" (p. 139), "at the same time remembering the courtesy and deference due . . . the differing opinions of others" (p. 141). At the same time the North should not give way to the vehemence of the South (pp. 141–42). The antislavery people should concern themselves with peacefully changing the hearts and minds of proslavery southerners. With this dialogue they could do much to help the slave (p. 11).

Channing, while not an abolitionist, denounced deliberate and systematic efforts to deprive them of freedom of speech and of the press. This persecution had included stoning, destruction of presses, and disruption of meetings. Abolitionists had firmly and fearlessly supported free speech and a free press. The protectors of liberty were not those who claimed and exercised rights that no one assails or who spoke well turned compliments on the fourth of July (pp. 158–59). The resolve of the abolitionists "to suffer, to die, rather than surrender their dearest liberties, taught the lawless, that they had a foe to contend with" (p. 160). But Channing did not have complete faith in democracy, since "the multitude, if once allowed to dictate or proscribe subjects of discussion, would strike society with spiritual blindness, and death" (p. 161).

Concerning the accusation that the abolitionists endangered the Union, Channing asked how? The only reply he had received was that they exasperate the South. He asked, "Is it a crime to exasperate men? . . . Can the calmest book be written on Slavery, without producing the same effect?" [p. 166]

On the other hand, abolitionist "writings, he thought, had been blemished by a spirit of intolerance, sweeping censure, and rash, injurious judgment. . . . Abolitionism, in the main, has spoken in an intolerant tone, and in this way had repelled many good minds, given great advantage to its opponents, and diminished the energy and effect of its appeals (167). Further, their intolerance toward the slaveholder has awakened toward him sympathy rather than indignation, and weakened the effect of their just invectives against the system which he upholds (p. 170).

Since the rich and fashionable belong to the same caste as the slaveholder, Channing saw that they were more apt to sympathize with him rather than the slave. "The slave is too low, too vulgar . . ." (p. 171). Then in the commercial class there are those who "have profitable connections with the slaveholder, which must not be endangered by expressions of sympathy with the slave. Gain is their god. . . . [T]o such, the philanthropy, which would break every chain, is fanaticism, or a pretence" (p. 172). Another class who opposes all antislavery movements is that of the conservatives. Channing also denounced politicians who only knew the law of expediency and who were "prepared to kiss the feet of the South for" votes (p. 173).

Concerning newspapers, Channing thought that they eschewed unpopular causes that would "thin their subscription-lists." Therefore, conscientious people supported their own organs which were more vitriolic. Experience should teach "that persecution is not the way to put down opinions" (p. 178).

Channing saw how the South had changed in regard to slavery. Once, it was acknowledged as an evil. "Now it is proclaimed to be a good" (p. 143). His support of the antislavery movement was welcomed by Birney, who endeavored to broaden the abolitionist appeal. Garrison, on the other hand, accused Channing of plagiarizing the "despised" abolitionists and feared that his influence would disturb the purity of the movement.[10]

VI *Frederick Douglass*

The unfairness of slavery was perhaps best expressed by the great black leader, Frederick Douglass. As an escaped slave turned abolitionist, Douglass completely refuted the argument of southern proslavery advocates that northern abolitionists knew little of the peculiar institution. His emotionally charged attacks on slavery expanded the abolitionist movement. Yet because he advocated political action, Garrison broke with him.[11] The passage which follows from Douglass's 4 July 1852 speech in Rochester, New York, is extremely persuasive and easily puts the proslavery forces in an untenable position:

Is it not astonishing that, while we are ploughing, planting and reaping, using all kinds of mechanical tools, erecting houses, constructing bridges, building ships, working in metals of brass, iron, copper, silver and gold; that while we are reading, writing and cyphering, acting as clerks, merchants and secretaries, having among us lawyers, doctors, ministers, poets, authors, editors, orators and teachers; that, while we are engaged in all manner of enterprises common to other men, digging gold in California, capturing the whale in the Pacific, feeding sheep and cattle on the hill-side, living, moving, acting, thinking, planning, living in families as husbands, wives and children, and, above all, con[f]essing and worshipping the Christian's God, and looking hopefully for life and immortality beyond the grave, we are called upon to prove that we are men. . . . What, am I to argue that it is wrong to make men brutes, to rob them of their liberty, to work them without wages, to keep them ignorant of their relations to their fellow men, to beat them with sticks, to flay their flesh with the lash, to load their limbs with irons, to hunt them with dogs, to sell them at auction, to sunder their families, to knock out their teeth, to burn their flesh, to starve them into obedience and submission to their masters? Must I argue that a system thus marked with blood, and stained with pollution, is *wrong*? No! I will not.[12]

VII *Lysander Spooner*

The more radical reformers' attack on slavery as an institution led many conservative northerners to think that they were assailing property. Such northerners did not question the moral justification of holding property that had been declared legal by state law. Both the organized church in the North and most of the legal profession took an extremely weak position. At the same time the new abolitionist doctrine worked out by Lysander Spooner created new possibilities for antislavery action.[13] Spooner, a strong libertarian, questioned the constitutionality of slavery.[14] Law, he defined, "a *natural*, unalterable, universal principle, governing such object or thing." Any rule not permanent, universal, and inflexible was not law. There could be "no law but natural law":[15] Natural law . . . inasmuch as it recognizes the natural right of men to enter into obligatory contracts permits the formation of government. . . . But in order that the contract of government may be valid and lawful, it must purport to authorize nothing inconsistent with natural justice, and men's natural rights. It cannot lawfully authorize government to destroy or take from men their natural rights. [p. 8]

Spooner successfully questioned Massachusetts' requirement of three years of study before admission to the bar. He fought the Post Office by establishing a rival company. With the same enthusiasm he demolished the proslavery argument based on free persons and "all other persons" in the Constitution (p. 91).

Spooner argued that slavery was a national issue, not just a southern one. Because of it the slave states lagged behind the free states economically. His appeal in this respect was directed to the northern business community, which would thus benefit considerably from a free South. Massachusetts, he claimed, furnished during the Revolution more soldiers than all the six southern states together. The nation, as a political community, had a vital interest in the character and republicanism of each state government (p. 134). The free states were pulling their weight. They were sharing

the incalculable wealth produced by our inventions and labor-saving machinery, our steam engines, and cotton gins, and manufactured machinery of all sorts, and yet say at the same time that we have no interest, and that there is 'no propriety' in the constitutional guaranty of that personal freedom to the people of the south, which would enable them to return us some equivalent in kind. [p. 132]

VIII   Cassius M. Clay and John Gregg Fee

The South never became a solid proslavery camp. Tennessee produced Andrew Johnson who, supported by the east Tennesseeans, stayed with the Union during the Civil War. Missouri had a thriving Republican party, headed by Frank and Montgomery Blair. In Kentucky an abolitionist movement was led by Cassius M. Clay and John Gregg Fee. As a student at Yale, Clay, a son of a wealthy slaveholder, was influenced by Garrison and became acquainted with abolitionists and Free-Soilers. Returning to Kentucky, he supported gradual emancipation and opposed the inefficiency of the plantation system.[16] Clay credited Thomas Jefferson with believing that "the master must liberate the slave, or the slave will exterminate the master."[17] Slavery was the cause of the ruin of the noblest nations of antiquity. Clay claimed

Slavery is an evil to the slave, by depriving nearly three millions of men of the best gift of God to man—liberty. . . . Slavery is an evil to the master. It is utterly subversive of the Christian religion. It violates the great law upon which that religion is based. . . . It is the source of indolence, and destructive of all industry, which in times past among the wise has ever been regarded as the first friend of religion, morality, and happiness. The poor despise labor, because slavery makes it degrading. The mass of slaveholders are idlers.

It is the mother of ignorance. The system of common schools has not succeeded in a single slave state. Slavery and education are natural enemies. . . . It is opposed to literature, even in the educated classes.

It is destructive of all mechanical excellence. The free states build ships and steam cars for the nations of the world; the slave states import the handles for their axes—these primitive tools of the architect. . . .

It is antagonistic to the fine arts. . . . The manufactures of the slave as compared to those of the free states, are as one to four nearly. . . .

It impoverishes the soil and defaces the loveliest features of nature. . . .

It induces national poverty. Slaves consume more and produce less than freemen. Hence illusive wealth, prodigality, and bankruptcy, without the capability of bearing adversity, or recovering from its influence: then comes despair, dishonor, and crime.

It is an evil to the free laborer, by forcing him by the laws of competition, supply, and demand, to work for the wages of the slave—food and shelter. The poor, in the slave states, are the most destitute native population in the United States.

It sustains the public sentiment in favor of the deadly affray and the duel—those relics of a barbarous age.

It is the mother and the nurse of *Lynch law*, which I regard as the most horrid of all crimes, not even excepting patricide, which ancient legislators thought too impossible to be ever supposed in the legal code. If all the blood thus shed in the South could be gathered together, the horrid image which Emmett drew of the cruelty of his judges would grow pale in view of this greater terror.

Where all these evils exist, how can liberty, constitutional liberty, live? No indeed, it cannot and has not existed in conjunction with slavery. [pp. 203–05]

Clay's writings encouraged the Reverend John Gregg Fee to come to middle Kentucky. The rugged terrain there made the use of slaves impractical. A native Kentuckian, Fee was involved in the establishment of Berea College which became an "oasis of antislavery and democratic education."[18]

In 1848 Fee published an antislavery manual in which he called slavery a common enemy of religion, virtue, and knowledge. The federal government had declared the foreign slave trade piracy, and domestic slavery was "in nature, practice and crime, the same, . . ."[19] His manual was designed to awaken the conscience of the slaveholder. He maintained that his argument was Bible based: "We appeal to the Bible because the apologists of slavery also appeal to it; and . . . by false interpretations, make it to support despotism of the grossest form" (p. viii).

Fee compared the wealth and intelligence of the free and slave states. Since the South had better soil and climate, slavery was the cause of the difference. The people in the free states did not have the problem with "slothful, unskilful, wasteful laborers" (p. 166). They were not in constant fear of insurrection. Fee asked, "Is it not better that a few masters should suffer small inconvenience, rather than that three millions of our fellow beings should suffer inconvenience, a thousand fold greater, and the robbery of their dearest rights? . . . The non-slaveholders suffer a great inconvenience in getting free laborers; because slavery makes labor disreputable, and keeps away the free laborer" (p. 166).

IX   Hinton Helper

Coming from North Carolina yeoman farmer stock, Hinton Helper battled against the domination of the South by plantation aristocrats. His purpose in writing *The Impending Crisis* (1857) was to make a vicious attack on their labor supply. Free labor, he maintained, was "far more respectable, profitable, and productive than slave labor."[20] His solution was to expel the entire slave population from the United States. To prove his thesis concerning the superiority of free labor he used the compendium of the census of 1850 to contrast the economic prosperity of northern and southern states. The use of his book as campaign literature by the Republican party in 1860 enabled him to be widely read in the North and hated in the South.[21]

Writing with an acid pen, Helper first compared the progress and prosperity of the North with the inertness and imbecility of the South. His first comparison was between Virginia and New York, first in 1791 and then in 1852. New York exports in 1791 stood at $2,505,456, as compared to Virginia's $3,130,865. By 1852 New York exported $87,484,456, compared to Virginia's $2,724,657. Other statistics were similar:[22] "The reason for why the North had surpassed the South could be traced on to common source, and there find solution in the most hateful and horrible word, that was ever incorporated into the vocabulary of human economy—Slavery!" (p. 25).

Helper argued that the planters formed an oligarchy. "Their intrigues and tricks of legerdemain" were most familiar; ". . . in vain might the world be ransacked for a more precious junto of flatterers and cajolers" (p. 42). It was insulting to one's intelligence to hear them "pervert the sacred principles of liberty, and turn the curse of slavery into a blessing" (pp. 42–43).

If poor whites dared to speak out, particularly on the issue of slavery, they were "obliged to become heroes, martyrs, or exiles" (p. 44). Not only that but "they are cajoled into the notion that they are the freest, happiest and most intelligent people in the world, and are taught to look with prejudice and disapprobation upon every new principle or progressive movement" (p. 45).

Thus, Helper saw clearly the opposition in the South to the various reforms. He also saw the oligarchy misleading the South insofar as agriculture in the North was concerned, of perpetuating a myth of "an uninterrupted barren waste" (p. 46). Further, the oligarchy sought for the slave states a "yoke of a worse tyranny than that which overshadowed them under the reign of King George the Third" (p. 116).

The only way a man could be a "true patriot" was to first become an abolitionist (p. 116). Slavery was "a great social and political evil, *a sin and a crime*" (p. 118). Slaveholders were "arrogant demagogues" who taught the farmers, mechanics, and workingmen of the South to "hate the abolitionists . . . your best and only true friends" (p. 120). There was no neutral ground (p. 121). The planters argued that slavery could not be abolished "without infringing on the rights of property." Helper refused to recognize that a human being could be property. For the slaveholders to pass laws for the abolition of slavery, one might just as well expect highwaymen to clamor for a universal law against traveling (pp. 155–56).

In the 1856 election, according to Helper, tens of thousands of southerners desired to vote for the Republican nominee, John C. Fremont, a nonslaveholding southerner. They were intimidated by the oligarchy. "Slavery tolerates no freedom of the press—no freedom of speech—no freedom of opinion" (p. 410).

In conclusion, Helper predicted that in alliance with the "intelligent free voters of the North," in 1860 the southern nonslaveholders would elect either John C. Fremont, Cassius M. Clay, or James G. Birney, all native southerners, to the presidency. Then the same alliance would next elect William H. Seward, Charles Sumner, or some other nonslaveholder of the North (p. 413).

Helper's book had an immediate impact in the North. Because of his extreme position, his analysis and remedy failed to achieve reform in the South; then, too, few of the nonslaveholding whites read *The Impending Crisis*.[23]

X *Samuel M. Wolfe*

Self-designated intellectual Samuel M. Wolfe, a Virginian, produced a stirring emotional rebuff to Helper's analysis.[24] Wolfe accused Helper of palming off prejudice as historical fact. There was "manifest unfairness" in his selection of statistics. This was typical of the "Black Republicans." The South, if forced by the North, could establish a separate and independent government, successfully trading with the commercial world. Wolfe asserted, "Cotton is King." To support that statement he quoted J. D. B. DeBow: "It is the cotton-bale that makes the treaties of the world, and binds over the nations to keep the peace."[25]

Wolfe claimed that slavery was supported by both the Bible and the Constitution.

And these rights we intend to enjoy, or to a man we will die, strung along Mason & Dixon's line with our faces looking North. Leave us in the peaceable possession of our slaves, and our Northern neighbors may have all the paupers and convicts that pour in upon us from European prisons, the getters up of "hunger meetings" at the North and the propagators of the most irreligious and impious "isms" of the day. The productive wealth of the South, her agricultural and mineral resources, her population and extent of territory, are greatly underrated by the politicians of the North, and the reckless agitators of the slavery question, such as Seward, Chase, Giddings & Co. [p. 74]

He warned that the South on short notice could

raise, equip, and maintain in the field, a larger force than any power on earth can send against her: men, too, brought up on horseback and in active life, with guns in their hands—men who will not desert their colors, as some of the Northern men have done in Mexico and elsewhere! [p. 75]

XI *Louis Schade*

Louis Schade, a German-American Democratic political writer and lawyer, had participated in the 1848 Revolution in Germany while a law student at the University of Berlin. Condemned to death by the Prussian government, he escaped to the United States. In 1856

Senator Stephen A. Douglas persuaded him to edit the *National Demokrat*, a German-language newspaper owned by the senator in Chicago.[26] Unlike Carl Schurz and other antislavery German-Americans, Schade was a strong supporter of the southern position on slavery.

In *A Book for the "Impending Crisis!" Appeal to the Common Sense and Patriotism of the People of the United States, "Helperism" Annihilated! The "Irrepressible Conflict" and Its Consequences* (1860), Schade made an impassioned attack on Helper's thesis. The German-American editor accused the abolitionists of being the greatest enemies of the slaves. There was an element of truth in this since Helper was a strong racist. Schade also charged unfairly that Helper's book was directed "against the free white laborers, mechanics, and merchants of the north."[27]

Schade claimed that "he would rather see the negro free. . . . But history . . . shows too clearly that the negro is incapable of taking care of himself; that he must be cared for, if he is to emerge out of his African barbarism . . ." (p. 56).

He pointed out the importance of cotton in foreign trade, particularly for the British market. He emphasized that the welfare of both England and the United States depended upon the cultivation of cotton by slave labor: "What would this country be without the two hundred millions of dollars of cotton annually produced? Where would be our greatness, our prosperity, as a commercial nation? Let the people of the North answer these questions for themselves" (p. 72).

XII *Summary*

All the antislavery writers viewed slavery as an evil institution. Most of them were crusaders who invariably depicted the worst aspects of the "peculiar institution." They generally ignored working conditions in factories of the North. They were able to see beyond the stereotype of the ignorant, lazy, immoral childlike slave that emerged from most proslavery writing. The antislavery writers also clearly exposed the inconsistency of proclaiming liberty and freedom, as John C. Calhoun and his followers did, and supporting slavery. The antislavery movement was the first great reform movement of the United States.

CHAPTER 5

Party Battles 1852–1860

I Demise of the Whigs

IN the 1840s mass immigration, particularly of the Irish, caused grave concern to native American workers. With the Democrats monopolizing the foreign vote, a number of Whig politicians took a nativist attitude. In Louisiana in 1841 the more extremist nativists formed their own third party, known as the Native American party. Since Louisiana seemingly was more lax than New York in the enforcement of immigration laws, New Orleans and the Mississippi Valley cities had an influx of Irish, the more unfortunate of whom filled almshouses, jails, and hospitals. Other "undesirables" operated as pickpockets, thieves, and beggars. The Native American party spread to the North, and in 1844 elected a mayor of New York and six members of Congress. However, its poor showing in 1848 ended its career.[1]

The same year the European Revolution of 1848 increased immigration. Among these were the political refugees. Also, the conviction grew among native Americans that English and Irish authorities were shipping potato famine victims to the United States. In 1851 two events occurred: immigration peaked at 600,000, and a papal nuncio arrived in the United States. Intense religious prejudice combined with economic, social, and political pressures to cause the rise of the Supreme Order of the Star Spangled Banner, better known as the Know-Nothings.[2]

To project the Whig point of view the *American Whig Review* had appeared first in 1845. Its chief political writer was former New York congressman Daniel D. Barnard. After writing the majority of its political articles, he left the magazine in 1850 to become minister to Prussia. After this the *American Whig Review* printed articles on both sides of the slavery question, antagonizing North and South alike. It also temporarily espoused nativism. The editor-in-chief in 1852, its final year, was probably journalist George W. Peck. The political articles in it were usually anonymous.[3]

Going into the election of 1852 the Whigs held the presidency. The rise of nativism temporarily strengthened the party, since many Catholics and recently arrived immigrants tended to be Democrats. Joining native American workers in making the nativist issue a major one were a number of rural Protestants.[4] At the Whig convention delegates had a choice among the incumbent president, Millard Fillmore; the legendary spokesman of New England and business, Daniel Webster; and a bona fide War of 1812 and Mexican War hero, General Winfield Scott. Having had phenomenal success with war heroes, the Whigs selected Scott, and the *American Whig Review* as late as September was quite optimistic: "The American people, as a whole, are Democratic in their sentiments. The Whig party have the policy and the feeling of American democracy; the Democrats the name and the vices."[5]

The *Whig Review* took issue with the claim of the Democrats in their platform that their policy was "To resist monopolies and all exclusive legislation for the benefit of the few at the expense of the many." The same policy was a fundamental maxim of the Whig party, and "the Democrats have stolen our best thunder. . . ." The Whigs, for example, favored navigational improvements for the West to "place the Western producer and trader" in a more equitable position with the "farmers, merchants and traders of the Atlantic States. . . ." The Whigs were in favor of education and land reform. They also favored ending "the monopoly of manufactures retained by the capitalists of Great Britain," and interposing a barrier of legal protection between the American democracy and the mercantile aristocracy of Great Britain (p. 195).

The Whig's golden opportunity was partially destroyed by General Scott's inept campaign. Further, southern Whigs deserted, fearing that Scott, a staunch Unionist, might be inclined, as Taylor had been, to favor antislavery Whig politicians.[6] A coalition Union movement following the Compromise of 1850 fell apart when Union Democrats sent delegations to the national party convention. Union Whigs were stranded; some drifted back to the Whig party and reluctantly supported Scott, who carried only Tennessee and Kentucky of the slave states.[7]

The *Whig Review* lamented the outcome of the election. "It is proved that military popularity alone, even when united with the highest civil and diplomatic qualities, will not elect a President."[8] Pierce, the magazine saw as an unknown elected by "the machinations of a powerful combination of office seekers" (p. 506). Thus "the office of President is no longer the reward of merit . . ." (p. 507). It traced the defeat of the Whigs back to President Taylor's death which reversed the administration's policy, causing the popular tide to turn.

The great victory achieved by the measures of compromise, by which the State of California was admitted to the Union, with a protest against the extension of slavery, and by which the rights of the South were on all sides limited, and at the same time protected and established within their proper limits, may be regarded as the concluding stage and last scene of the reaction. The compromise measures were carried by the votes and influence, for the most part, of Northern men and Whigs; and the great leader and representative [Clay] of the Whig party was the originator and principal defender. His death, and that of Mr. Webster, seems to be the conclusion of a cycle. Democracy commences anew with its peculiar expansive policy; the Whigs are again thrown into opposition; a new war has begun. It will pass in all probability through a series of changes, alternating victory and defeat, and terminating again, as heretofore, in the election of a President, whose executive policy will antagonize the expansive energy of the Northern and Southern aggressionists and interventionists. [p. 510]

II *Know-Nothing Movement*

After the 1852 election the Whig party disintegrated. Making a strong bid to become the new second party, the Know-Nothing movement adopted the American label. For a short time it was more successful in cities and towns of the East and the South than the Whig party had ever been. Much of its advocacy came from Protestant workers, who formerly had been staunch Jacksonian Democrats. Massachusetts, highly industrialized and the most densely populated state, soon became the chief stronghold of the Know-Nothings.[9] The leader of the Bay State's nativists was Senator Henry Wilson. As a child Wilson had been indentured as a farm hand for ten years. He then became a cobbler and next a successful shoe manufacturer. A Free-Soiler in 1848 he joined the American party in 1854.[10] Later he described the birth and growth of the Know-Nothing movement:

In the year 1853, a secret Order was organized by a few men in the city of New York. Its professed purpose was to check foreign influence, purify the ballot-box, and rebuke all efforts to exclude the Bible from the public schools. The dissatisfaction in the ranks of the old parties, growing out of the attempted repeal of the Missouri compromise in the winter of 1854, caused it to increase in that city with wonderful rapidity, and to spread into other cities, towns, and States. The disorganization of parties, when that compromise was abrogated, crowded its secret Councils and it rapidly spread over the Northern States. Hundreds of thousands who cared less for its avowed principles and purposes than for the higher claims of justice and humanity, and had little faith in its permanency, were willing to use its machinery to disrupt the Whig and Democratic parties, in the confident hope that, out of the disorganized masses, there would come a great political party antagonistic to the dominating influences of the Slave Power.[11]

The Boston-based *The Know-Nothing and American Crusader* in September 1854 optimistically asserted:

Our opponents very naturally prophecy that the American movement will be of transient duration. They can't like us, and therefore wish us—further. But nothing is more certain than that the American cause and organization will live out all others in the country. It has a broad foundation. It has a deep hold upon the affections and convictions of the people. . . . The American cause is not the result of a mere excitement—not the growth of a moment.[12]

The *Crusader* proclaimed the doctrine of jobs for native Americans only. It appealed to employers to hire only "American" mechanics and "American" laborers. On immigration laws it asked the question:

. . . should there be any Naturalization laws at all? Our opinion decidedly is, there should not. . . . It isn't safe to give this citizenship. . . . It is simply transferring political power . . . into the hands of foreigners. . . . They cannot understand the principles of our government, the measures or men which their votes act upon. Directed by base and intriguing men, they put down the very things it is for the general good should be sustained. . . . America for Americans. . . .[13]

Books on the papal conspiracy were offered for sale. At the same time the *Crusader* announced that the Irish potato famine was over and that they should go home. Some were doing just that. One anonymous poet had as his theme the Irish migration:

The Paupers
by Ichabod Crane, Jr.

I

The paupers came down, like the wolf on the fold
On the land that was teeming with plenty and gold:
Filth, famine and pestilence ushered them o'er
From "ould country" hovels, to cumber our shore.

II

And here came the beggar, grown hoary in crime,
And sturdy young vagrants from "Green Erin's" clime,
And fat "Father Murphy's" flock over in squads
To drill them in voting—for Rome and her Gods.

III

Like leaves of the forest, when summer is green,
That host at the ballot-box oft have been seen,
Like leaves of the forest, when autumn hath past,
That host shall be routed and scattered at last.

IV

Alas for their stratagems, priest-craft and wiles,
Alas for their voters from classic "St. Giles":
No "bell, book or candles" nor mitre, nor crown,
Can keep Popery up, or put liberty down.

V

For the rally of freemen was borne on the blast,
It was heard in the camp of the foe as it passed;
And "Johnny of York" has gone home to his master
To learn how to meet this unthought of disaster.

VI

The sons of the soil have arisen in might,
All girded for battle, for "God and the Right."
The Bible our watchword—the ballot our sword,
We will conquer old Rome, by the help of the Lord.[14]

The Satanic Plot, or Awful Crimes of Popery in High and Low Places by a Know Nothing continued the attack on the pope and the Catholic Church:

We are living in singular times—times for which our prophets, sibyls, and Kings have waited long and desired most ardently. The world seems to have been awakened from a long sleep, to consider its mission and enter upon its high destiny. Among the movements of the times is the great awakening to the evils and designs of popery. This politico-religious power has had more influence upon the world's history than almost any other, and for twelve centuries has been the most malignant foe of God and man.[15]

The author of the *Satanic Plot* claimed that the papacy was now in its dotage, defended by the bayonets of foreign troops. With increasing weakness in Europe the Catholic Church was trying to recoup in

the United States at the expense of "our civil and religious liberties."
It would spread among us "the dark pall of barbarism and superstition." The vast immigration, headed by priests, presented an immediate danger. In addition to the religious threat, from immigration came "nearly four fifths of the beggary, two thirds of the pauperism, and more than three fifths of the crimes . . ." (p. 6).

Antislavery activism of a minority of the northern Know-Nothings caused the stigma of being an antislavery party in the South. Following the defeat of the American party in Virginia in the spring of 1855, the Know-Nothing National Council met in Philadelphia in June. Shortsighted southern politicians, together with their northern sympathizers, were successful in pledging the American party to slavery, causing fifty northern antislavery delegates to walk out. Eventually, led by Senator Wilson, they would join the Republicans.[16]

Democratic writer and German immigrant, Louis Schade, answered the Know-Nothing charges in the campaign of 1856. *The Immigration into the United States from a Statistical and National-Economical Point of View* held that

if immigration had been cut off in 1790, our population in 1850 would have been about what it was in 1820. Immigration, then, has put us thirty years forward in this important element of national prosperity. Our increase in all departments of national progress has been in the exact ratio of our increase in population. Whilst the latter has increased sixfold, our commercial exports have increased, in the same period, eightfold, and our imports threefold.[17]

Schade asserted that an effect of the Know-Nothing movement had been a sharp decrease in immigration in 1855. Immigrants came to the United States, "just as much for political freedom as material well-being." The people of the United States could

prevent immigration and prohibit it if they will. . . . But the loss of the laborious immigrant will soon be felt. . . . most of the immigrants wended their way to the prairies of the Far West, buying from the government with their own money the public lands, in order to wrest a livelihood from the bosom of mother earth. Their labors have enriched not only the cultivator, but the country and the native-born children. Others again remained in the great Atlantic cities, where their herculean energies have been employed in the erection of public works. Men of genius, artists, scholars, came with this tide of immigration; and . . . they have . . . vastly contributed to the intellectual stores of this country. (pp. 13–14)

Schade felt that the Know-Nothings "would degrade the emigrant to the low position of an East Indian pariah, or a Russian serf . . . to dig canals and build railroads . . . to act as hewer of wood and drawer of water to those who falsely call themselves superior beings" (p. 14).

The appeal of this Democratic political writer was more to the self-interest of the white laborers than of the humanitarian approach. He warned that the Know-Nothings in free states were attempting "to elevate the negro to the political rights and privileges of the whites" (p. 14).

Since, according to Schade, there was "not a single foreign-born member in Congress," he belittled the cry of the Know-Nothings: "Americans must rule America!" (p. 14). He asked how many Know-Nothings could trace their lineage back to the revolution:

Are not at least two-thirds of their number descendants of those who arrived in the country since 1790? Was not, in New York, even their candidate for governor a son of a foreigner? Are not, with the only exception of two, all the 148 or 149 Know-nothings of the New York State legislature sons of foreign parents? . . . the warfare of Know-nothingism is against the principles on which our Revolution was started and was consummated—against the policy engrafted upon our constitution. [p. 15]

III   Election of 1856

The American party, badly split on the issue of slavery, was not destined to become a major party in 1856. That place would be usurped by a combination of various factions that coalesced in opposition to the Kansas-Nebraska Act in 1854. The origin of the Republican party was in the grass roots of the Midwest. Abraham Lincoln, its greatest leader, would not join it until 1856. In the presidential campaign the Democrats would emphasize how safe and conservative their candidate James Buchanan was and how radical and dangerous John C. Fremont and the "Black Republicans" were.[18] Included in their campaign literature was Words of Counsel to Men of Business by a Man of Business.

We invite the working and business man. . . . Let him observe the words of peaceful and conservative wisdom with which JAMES BUCHANAN speaks of the hateful subject of slavery and sectional discord. They are earnest. They are emphatic. They are precise. They reflect the deliberate intent with which he approaches the discharge of the great duty upon him—that of a National President of the United States. . . . [W]hat industry most needs,—what the merchant and farmer, the mechanic and manufacturer, most require— stability, steadiness, repose. What a blessing beyond calculation it will be, to have an administration for four years, during which, by the mere force of personal example, no word of acrimony shall be uttered on the subject of Domestic Slavery, and the nation's evil passions may be at rest![19]

The pamphlet emphasized that the Democratic convention at Cincinnati had representation from "every State of the Union, North, South, East, and West." Of the southern states only Virginia was represented in the Republican Convention in Philadelphia. Therefore, that party was a sectional movement. The Democratic party was for those who love the Union (p. 6).

Concerning the dire consequences of a Republican victory, Man of Business warned:

The election of an Abolition President breaks the Union into pieces, and Pennsylvania becomes a frontier, with the ragged edges of a frontier, with questions of boundary, of runaways, of aggression and resistance, of trouble of every kind; and Philadelphia and Pittsburg, neither of them fifty miles from the dividing line, not as they now are, great circulators of trade and manufactures through the South and West, reduced to doubtful frontier towns, with markets dependent on foreign and uncertain legislation. [p. 8]

The Democratic Hand-Book, compiled by Mich W. Cluskey of Washington, echoed the same theme as the pamphlet directed at businessmen. Further, the "Black Republicans" were compared with the antiwar disunionists in 1812. Cluskey mentioned that there existed in New England a conspiracy "to effect a dissolution of the Union at every hazard, and to form a separate Confederacy."[20]

The supporters of Fremont evaluated the election results quite differently. Following the narrow victory of Buchanan in the triangular race, the Republican Association of Washington, in an address to their fellow Republicans of the country at large, called the Democrats the proslavery party and its victory one of sectionalism. They claimed that the Republican party had been a sudden gathering of concerned people rather than a well organized party, that it was obstructed by a secret order which had a stronghold on national prejudices, that the Democrats had the united support of the South and the federal government. Yet, despite all this, the Republicans won in eleven free states, containing one half of the country's population.[21] The Republicans "know the ambition, the necessities, the schemes of the slave power." Their duty was action through the press and the ballot box. They correctly saw that Buchanan would not support a free Kansas, despite the fact that nineteen twentieths of the free state people and "perhaps more than half" of the slave state people were opposed to the extension of slavery (p. 536).

Putnam's Magazine, in its December issue, viewed the outcome of 1856 as a Pyrrhic victory for the Democrats. It correctly evaluated the demise of the American party. The Republican party had received a temporary setback:

. . . the Democratic, now the pro-slavery party, has gained its candidates, but damaged its cause; . . . the Republicans have lost their candidates, but furthered their cause; . . . the Americans, composed of the fragments of two old and decayed factions, have lost both candidates and cause . . . seemingly, forever. . . . The ruin of one party, the temporary check of another, and the doubtful ascendancy of the third, is what we read in the significant events of November.[22]

The article pointed out the heavy losses of the Democrats in New York, New England, and nearly the entire northwestern region. They were saved elsewhere in the North by the diversion caused by the Know-Nothings. Four years previously, in winning with Pierce, their ascendency had been undisputed:

They might have retained that ascendency, if they had adhered to their ancient principles, and not abandoned themselves to the guidance of a few demagogues, working in the interests of a special, and by no means acceptable class. But in an evil hour they suffered themselves; and, by the repeal of the Missouri Compromise, which was uncalled for by any necessity, political or local—by the long series of outrages which accompanied the enforcement of the Kansas-Nebraska act. . . . [T]heir only salvation was the slaveholding interests of the South, and the lingering prejudices in favor of that interest, which still maintained a feeble hold upon the North. [pp. 648–49]

Python, writing in *DeBow's Review*, observed different demagogues. He predicted that the Know-Nothings would be absorbed by the "Black Republicans" who in turn would gain acceptance in the free states. His explanation was the principle of agrarianism.

The mind conversant with those great struggles of antiquity that originated in the agrarian proclivities of no-property classes, always clashing with the interests of property-holders, invariably leading to the desecration of law, and, ultimately, to the disruption of constitutional government, discovers in them the prototype of all that now exists, and all, I fear, that must follow in our Confederacy. . . . From the nature of things with us—the Southern States being slaveholding and agricultural, and withholding from their slaves the right of suffrage and all participation in government, whilst the Northern States hold no slaves, are commercial and manufacturing, and extend to all alike the right of suffrage and participation in government—it has come to pass on the one hand, that the citizens of the South are, for the most part, property-holders and conservative in their political character, while on the other hand, those of the North, for the most part, hold no property. . . .[23]

Thus the fight was between the southern property holders and the day-laboring, landless multitude of the North. These included the public education advocates, women righters, and those for laws protecting tenants. "Under the action of universal suffrage, how could the legislative bodies of the North avoid engrafting on their statute books the measures of agrarianism?" (pp. 114–15). Here was a bold repudiation of Jacksonian democracy coming from a leading southern periodical. Python predicted the victory of the Republicans in 1860 (p. 129).

IV   *Election of 1860*

Buchanan's administration was a stormy one. Reaction from the Dred Scott decision, trouble in Kansas, and the John Brown episode at Harpers Ferry widened the gulf between the free and slave states. In the March 1860 issue of *DeBow's Review* Python presented a viewpoint supported by many proslavery southerners: "The designs of Black-republicanism, and the issues of 1860, in their consequences to the South, the Constitution, and the Union, cannot be exaggerated. They involve alike the integrity of the Democratic Party, the preservation of the confederacy, and the continuation of the republic. The triumph of Black-republicanism must be the termination of constitutional government and liberty, and the beginning of empire with dictatorial tyranny, or of disunion and civil war."[24]

Python perceived the rival party to be a combination of Black Republicanism and the Know-Nothing movement. He emphasized the support that immigrants and Catholics in general had given the Democratic party: "Puritanism! Americanism! Abolitionism! Agrarianism! these are the four fundamental elements of the Black-republican organization, and so long as that organization remains a political power, these elements must vitalize and direct its motions. Each distinctively recognizes in the principles of Catholicity its own antagonism" (p. 270).

The particular bête noire of Python was Senator William H. Seward of New York. The possibility of his being the Republican candidate for president presented an extremely galling exigency for the *DeBow's Review* political commentator (p. 271).

At the same time the *Political Text-Book, or Encyclopedia*, edited by M. W. Cluskey, postmaster of the United States House of Representatives, charged that the Republican party had the support of the Abolition party.[25]

In preparation for the crucial election, the *National Democratic Quarterly Review*, edited by Thomas B. Florence, a veteran doughface congressman from Philadelphia, made its appearance in 1859 as a pro-Buchanan administration organ. Florence was also the owner of the *Philadelphia Argus*.[26] Published in Washington, the *Democratic Review* saw the history of the United States as a "political contest between two rival parties."[27] Florence traced the country's progress from the colonies of New England, where states rights originated, through the Constitution, the War of 1812, to 1859, emphasizing the support that the Democrats had given the federal union (pp. 8–18).

The *Democratic Review* had lavish words of praise for Buchanan: "The great events of his Administration . . . have been the quiet and peaceful settlement of the Utah and Kansas questions; the breaking up of the unlawful military expeditions against the States of Central America; and the successful adjustment, through the Secretary of State, of the *questio vexata* of the right of search" (p. 73).

It also labeled the Republican party the Abolition party (p. 191), and claimed that "nothing for the peace, welfare, or happiness of the negro would be conduced by his liberation" (p. 193). Coming from the Cradle of Liberty was seemingly irrelevant to Florence, who despite little education was a self-appointed expert on African history and culture: "Had the negro been intended by the Creator for an elevation to an equality with the white man, his nature would not have been so formed that he can only reach and maintain his highest development in a state of servitude."[28]

With the Democrats rent by interparty strife, Florence pleaded for party unity, pointing out the dangers of a Republican victory.

. . . we *must* be united if we want to carry the victory next November. Our southern friends ought never to forget that the battle will be fought on northern ground—that their northern brethren will have to meet the enemy—for there are no Republicans in the southern States. Therefore, the northern Democracy, being the avaunt-guard, they ought to be encouraged, strengthened, and supported by the South. The Republicans have ill-treated the South since their first appearance. Fanaticism has blinded their eyes, and ignorance of existing circumstances and facts have induced not a few of them to operate against their own interests and welfare. They are the avowed enemies of the South, and no man doubts that, if they should get in the ascendant, they will carry out their nefarious schemes and ruin this country. [p. 399]

The *Democratic Review* claimed that the right of Congress to inhibit slavery in the territories was no longer a practical issue (p. 412). The true objectives of the Republicans were very clearly enunciated by Lincoln in his debates with Douglas in 1858. There, Lincoln affirmed, "A house divided against itself cannot stand" (p. 413). William H. Seward followed in the footsteps of Lincoln with the statement that "It is an irrepressible conflict between opposing and enduring forces, and it means that the United States must and will, sooner or later, become either entirely a slaveholding nation or entirely a free labor nation" (p. 414).

For president the *Democratic Review* supported John C. Breckinridge, the candidate of the southern wing of the Democratic party. Florence held him to be the "national, conservative candidate of the old Jacksonian Democracy":[29] "His election—and we look forward to that with cheerful hope—. . . and in the never-failing devotion to his country which shall mark his administration will be witnessed a withering rebuke to his enemies. We shall behold in him such a President . . . fit to wield the sceptre which Jackson, . . . Polk, . . . Pierce and Buchanan have left, untarnished and unbent. . . . And the great, the honored, the legitimate Democratic party shall be preserved in its ancient integrity" (p. 619).

A pamphlet issued by the National Democratic Executive Committee (Breckinridge) echoed Florence's *Democratic Review*. Titled *The Great Issue To Be Decided in November Next! Shall the Constitution and the Union Stand or Fall, Shall Sectionalism Triumph?: Lincoln and His Supporters* it asked: "What does it all mean? *The dissolution of the American Union, the emancipation of the Southern slaves, and the reduction of the Southern States and Southern men into the abject position of colonies and vassals.* This is the "bloody goal" at which Black Republicanism strives. . . . Let the conservative men of the country now rally to the [National Democratic] standard, and it will meet, overthrow, and vanquish this dangerous enemy to the Republic, and give peace and security to the Union."[30]

Support of Breckinridge's candidacy for president was not limited in the North to party hacks who were pro-Buchanan administration. The *New York Herald*, edited by the able James Gordon Bennett, championed Breckinridge and derided the Republicans: "The Breckinridge and Lane ratification meeting has awakened the first echo from the popular heart, and given to the whole country the key note for the national bugles, and the true plan for the opening campaign. The contest is one of conservative resistance to the revolutionary and destructive schemes of the black republican fanatics and demagogues, and it is in the central, commercial, manufacturing and mining States that the people can be rallied. . . ."[31]

The *Herald* saw the critical area to be the "central and commercial States on the Southern border . . .":

On one side stands Lincoln, proclaiming the social, moral and political superiority of the North over the South, and calling upon men to enter into an "irrepressible conflict" for the complete and entire destruction of the Southern States. On the other hand we have Breckinridge proclaiming the equality and brotherhood of the States, the harmony of commerce and industry, the sacred and constitutional right of self-government, and urging upon the people to unite in their defence. [p. 4]

The *New York Times*, edited by Henry Raymond, saw the situation quite differently. Its editorial page stated that

The truth is, the Democrats do not hope for success, and few of them care for it. The party has become so thoroughly demoralized, all the great principles which formerly gave it power and popularity have so completely disappeared, that its leading members have no faith in its future, and no heart for its expiring struggles. . . . Mr. Buchanan has given the finishing touches to the degradation of his party, and has made respectable persons ashamed to confess that they ever belonged to it.[32]

Insofar as the Republicans were concerned, the *New York Herald* did not predict clear sailing for them. It quoted Thurlow Weed as advising them "not to be lulled into a false sense of security by the distracted condition of the democracy." The *Herald* reported the lack of enthusiasm of the Republicans as compared with the election of 1856.[33]

In August an abolitionist convention nominated Gerrit Smith for president, supporting the contention of editor Bennett that extreme antislavery Republicans would not support Lincoln. Bennett then predicted that "the revolt of the radical anti-slavery faction in New York of 1844, which defeated Henry Clay, will be repeated, and may produce a similar result in 1860."[34]

The *New York Daily-Tribune*, edited by Horace Greeley, saw the Republicans "united" and "working hard." The staunchly Republican editor reported their meetings well attended. Thus "with no desire to incite undue confidence," Greeley predicted the certain election of Lincoln.[35] The major issue of the campaign, according to the *Tribune's* editor, was whether "the interests and aspirations either of slave-breeding or of Free Labor must and will be paramount in our National policy; . . . Slave-breeding has had a long spell forward; Free labor is about to take its turn: Witness the Free Homestead and Tariff bills so nearly passed by Congress at its late session" (p. 4).

To support Lincoln's presidential bid, the Republican Congressional Committee issued a series of pamphlets in English and German. Among these was Abraham Lincoln's Cooper Union speech in New York, 27 February 1860. Prior to this occasion Lincoln had not been a front-runner for the presidency. Commenting on objections to a Republican victory, he told southerners at that time that

. . . you will not abide the election of a Republican President. In that supposed event, you say you will destroy the Union, and then, you say, the great crime of having destroyed it will be upon us! [Laughter.] That is cool. [Great laughter.] A highwayman holds a pistol to my ear, and mutters through his teeth, "Stand and deliver, or I shall kill you, and then you will be a murderer!" [Continued laughter.] To be sure, what the robber demanded of me—my money—was my own, and I had a clear right to keep it; but it was no more my own than my vote is my own; ["That's so," and applause;] and the threat of death to me, to extort my money, and the threat of destruction to the Union, to extort my vote can scarcely be distinguished in principle.[36]

This theme was reiterated by Sidney Edgerton, a Republican congressman from Ohio. Edgerton had been a member of the Free-Soil party in 1848 and in 1860 was serving his first term in Congress.[37] In a speech originally made in Congress and directed at the South, Edgerton thanked God that "we of the free states hold our rights by no such uncertain tenure as your will, but by virtue of the Constitution and our own manhood. Through the long night in which slavery has ruled this land, we have submitted to its iron sway; for years we have seen this Government all on the side of slavery! . . . [F]or a Northern man to say a word against the Union was rank treason. But at the South, how different! To advocate slavery was no crime, and to denounce the Union a positive virtue."[38]

The Ohio congressman warned against southerners speaking of dissolving the Union "as if it were a pastime—a holiday sport" (p. 7). Secession could not occur "without civil strife, and garments rolled in blood" (p. 7).

Rodolphus Holland Duell, a first term Republican congressman from Herkimer County in upstate New York, contrasted the Republican and Democratic parties in another pamphlet circulated by the Republican Executive Congressional Committee.[39] According to this leaflet, *Position of Parties*, the "Democratic party came into power sixty years ago, advocating . . . the equal rights of man."[40] Its "paramount doctrine . . . was the maintenance of personal rights against the encroachments of property" (p. 2). The Democratic party in the Pierce administration repealed the Missouri Compromise. In Buchanan's term of office the course of action of Jefferson and the founding fathers was abandoned (pp. 1–2). Slavery was now shaping national legislation, determining foreign policy, making presidents, and was "the power behind the throne . . ."(p. 2).

The Republican party did not come into "existence until the South, aided by Northern doughfaces, abrogated the Missouri Compromise" (p. 5). It was now the sole party that both adhered to Jeffersonian principles and opposed the extension of slavery. Duell denied that the Republicans were sectional: "The Democracy say we are so because our strength is at the North, and we are unable to carry any Southern State. . . . Tested by this rule, the Democratic party is likewise sectional; for it is a notorious fact, that every slave State is now Democratic, and every free State, save one, anti-Democratic" (pp. 4–5).

With Lincoln and the Republicans sweeping the free states, except for a split in New Jersey, James Gordon Bennett viewed the outcome with misgivings. His editorial was that of the loyal opposition:

. . . if the President-elect shall measure his steps by the landmarks of the constitution, and for the harmony of the country, we expect to stand by him. On the contrary, should he be led astray by the false lights of the "irrepressible conflict," we shall stick to him as we stuck to poor Pierce from the day of his departure from the line of duty until the day of his banishment from

Washington. To Abraham Lincoln now belongs the power of restoring or destroying the happy relations of peace and fraternity between the North and the South, and let us hope that he may prove equal to the crisis and the responsibility.[41]

V *Summary*

In the party battles of 1852–1860, the Democratic claim to Jacksonian democracy was under strong attack by opponents. After 1854, Republican writers were able with considerable success to claim identification with Jacksonian democracy, particularly with the image of Lincoln as the railsplitter and the strong figure who would hold the Union together. On the other hand, the Democratic party, badly split by the rift between the Free-Soil and proslavery people, moved more toward the old Whig conservative position, attempting to label the "Black Republicans" dangerous radicals. An effort to make permanent the American Know-Nothing party based on anti-Catholic and antiforeign prejudice failed. The election of 1860 was one of the few national elections that emphasized confrontation rather than compromise.

CHAPTER 6

Reconstruction and the New South

I Introduction

AN old chestnut is that wars not only fail to solve old problems but create new ones. The northern victory in the Civil War abolished slavery, saved the Union, and strengthened the rising industrial-business class. It also reduced the South to colonial status, economically and politically. Viewpoints, in antebellum days given strong support in the North, quickly made an appearance, as southern conservatives sought to reestablish the old alliance. *DeBow's Review* in December 1866 asserted that ". . . there has ever been too much Rationalism or Radicalism in the North, checked, balanced, and sufficiently counterpoised hitherto by the excessive Conservatism of the South; but that now, the South being powerless, Northern Radicalism will have full swing and dominion, and, unless the South is speedily restored to the Union, will, by rash innovations and radical changes, destroy our present form of government."[1]

However, the conservatism of the South, intertwined as it had been with proslavery concepts, was not to be in the midstream of American political thought in Reconstruction. Indeed, it would not be until one hundred years after the end of Reconstruction that a Deep South politician would be elected president. In addition, southern industry for many years would be hampered by discriminatory freight rates and the absentee landlord exploitation of Wall Street.

Even though not a single northern state outside of New England, except New York with a property requirement, in 1865 gave the franchise to the blacks, strong support in the North was given that summer to black voting in the former-Confederate states. E. L. Godkin in the *Nation* wrote "It is easy to see from the discussion which is going on on the question of reconstruction, that there is not in any quarter any opposition worthy of note to the abstract right of the negroes to the franchise."[2] Radical Reconstruction, utilizing the fourteenth and fifteenth amendments, enfranchised all black males, North and South. It also temporarily forged a Republican coalition as a viable second party in the South. When that party lost the old-line Whig element, alienated many of the ex-Unionists and was unable to keep the blacks from being disfranchised, it disintegrated into a patronage crowd reinforced by the hillbillies of Appalachia.

The so-called Compromise of 1877 was almost a complete victory for the South: Reconstruction was ended with the doctrine of states rights effectively replacing the fourteenth and fifteenth amendments. The southern wing of the Republican party lost control of the last three states that it controlled. However, again, as with the Civil War, old problems were not solved, just shelved.

The Reconstruction myth, that this was a period of corruption and abuse of government by blacks, scalawags, and carpetbaggers, was to a large extent influenced by the contemporary writings of Hilary Herbert, James S. Pike, and John Wallace. Honesty and dishonesty in Reconstruction politics were not monopolies of any particular faction or unique in United States history. After Reconstruction corruption would continue to plague the Democratic state governments in the South as earlier it had the Republican.

II *James S. Pike*

James S. Pike was one of the most influential northern journalists of his day. Associate editor and part owner of the *New York Tribune* during the 1850s, his antislavery views gained him the confidence of leading Republicans. As the North wearied of Reconstruction, Pike's book furnished invaluable arguments for sectional peace and racial harmony.[3] Describing a South Carolina Reconstruction legislature, Pike wrote:

A white community, that had gradually risen from small beginnings, till it grew into wealth, culture, and refinement, and became accomplished in all the arts of civilization . . . lies prostrate in the dust, ruled over by this strange conglomerate, gathered from the ranks of its own servile population. It is the spectacle of a society suddenly turned bottom-side up. . . .

In the place of this old aristocratic society stands the rude form of the most ignorant democracy that mankind ever saw, invested with the functions of government. It is the dregs of the population habilitated in the robes of their intelligent predecessors, and asserting over them the rule of ignorance and corruption, through the inexorable machinery of a majority of numbers. It is barbarism overwhelming civilization by physical force. It is the slave rioting in the halls of his master and putting that master under his feet. And, though it is done without malice and without vengeance, it is nevertheless none the less completely and absolutely done. [pp. 11–12]

III *John Wallace*

John Wallace, an escaped slave, born in North Carolina, came as a Union soldier to Florida during the Civil War. Injured in combat he remained after hostilities, finding employment as a school teacher on the plantation of the staunchly conservative Democrat, William D. Bloxham. Following a rather prominent career as one of the more progressive black leaders in Reconstruction, including service in the legislature, Wallace wrote *Carpetbag Rule* in Florida. Throughout the volume, starting with his approval of the Black Code of 1865, Wallace views the conservative Democrats as the really true friends of the blacks:[4]

It is true, that some of the laws passed by the legislature of 1865 seem to be very diabolical and oppressive to the freedmen, but when we consider the long established institution of slavery, and the danger to which the Southern whites imagined they might be subjected . . . any other people, under like circumstances, would have passed the same character of laws relative to the freedmen. Many of these laws we know . . . were passed only to deter the freedman from committing crime. [p. 35]

In addition, the white soldiers in military occupation "would abuse and maltreat the negro much worse than their former masters, who in many instances would have to interfere in his behalf, to save him from cruelty and injustice" (p. 37).

The Freedmen's Bureau, created by Congress to alleviate the tremendous problem of poverty in the South following the war, was thoroughly discredited by Wallace (pp. 40–42). Even though the idea was humanitarian and it was ". . . intended as a means of protection of the freedmen, and preparing them for the new responsibilities and privileges conferred, in the hands of bad men [it] proved, instead of a blessing, to be the worst curse of the race, as under it he was misled, debased and betrayed" (p. 40).

Wallace had high praise for the conservative Democrats:[5] ". . . colored men, however illiterate . . . [in] the Legislature, were listened to with marked attention by the Southern whites. . . . Not one word of criticism or ridicule was ever heard from one of them. . . .

The colored men who began to and continued to study professions found a ready friend in the Southern white man, who freely extended the right hand of fellowship to push the ex-slave to the zenith of his profession."[6]

The carpetbaggers emerged as the villains in his book: ". . . whenever a colored man would attempt to express his opinion against the questionable methods of the gang of adventurers who were in possession of the government, he would be whistled at, hissed at, and ridiculed, while on the floor of the legislative hall, and his language criticised, to compel him to desist from opposing them" (p. 324).

IV *Hilary A. Herbert*

In 1890 Confederate combat veteran Hilary A. Herbert of Montgomery, Alabama published a series of essays which summarized Reconstruction in each southern state. Lawyer, post-Reconstruction congressman, and secretary of the navy in the second administration of Cleveland, Herbert was a politician with considerable influence.[7] His book is a continuation of the old proslavery theme of the inferiority of the black. He also emphasized the barbarism of Africa.

Of all the races in the world the negro alone had been able to hold, always, a whole continent locked in the impenetrable mysteries of barbarism. . . . Brought from his native land, freed from native influences, as a slave he had greatly developed—he was kindly disposed, docile and faithful. He had cared for the women and children of the South, even when battles were being fought in which his freedom was at stake. For this the Southern people felt deeply grateful, yet they could not think that his training as a slave had fitted him to take part in the government of a state.[8]

That it was unlawful to teach the blacks to read he blamed on the abolitionists who had invited slave insurrections (p. 439). Since the first blacks arrived in 1619 and the fear of the abolitionists by southerners came after the Nat Turner Revolt in 1831, it is significant that Herbert does not explain the time discrepancy. Herbert was also against civil rights because they caused conflict between races (p. 439). He dismissed violence in Alabama by conservative Democrats as Republican propaganda "to invoke the aid of Federal authorities in" forthcoming elections (p. 64). The Republican party in the South, he maintained, was dominated by blacks. As a reaction to this and "to avert ruin white men united; and then came a struggle, the issue of

which was in all the States the same. . . . The race against which the
negro had allowed himself to be arrayed has never yet met its master.
It could not go down before the African" (p. 438). Now, with the
victory of the southern whites, the blacks were "far more prosperous
than they ever were under the rule of those who claimed to be their
especial friends" (p. 438).

V *Amnesty*

Amnesty in the United States has been a major issue only after two
conflicts: the Civil War and the Vietnamese conflagration. Other
wars, particularly the Revolutionary and the War of 1812 were divis-
ive; however, little support was given to pardoning the dissenters.
The Tories suffered loss of property, loss of status, and mass exile. The
"Blue Light" Federalists, after the War of 1812, were scarred by a
stigma which played a major role in the disintegration of their party.
The Civil War ended with the lenient surrender terms between
Grant and Lee at Appomattox. Citizenship was restored for most
ex-Confederates by means of the iron-clad oath, pardons by President Johnson, special enactments by Congress, and a general amnesty law that in 1872 reduced the number still proscribed to around
five hundred.[9]

Running counter to the theme of clasping hands were those southerners who claimed to be unreconstructed and those northerners
who looked on John Brown as a martyr and blamed Jefferson Davis for
the traumatic tragedy at Andersonville. For the former, Major Innes
Randolph, late of Jeb Stuart's staff, spoke expressively:

The Good Old Rebel

Oh, I'm a good old Rebel
Now that's just what I am;
For this "fair land of Freedom"
I do not care a damn.
I'm glad I fit against it—
I only wish we'd won
And I don't want no pardon
For anything I've done.
. . . .

> I hate the Yankee nation,
> And everything they do,
> I hates the Declaration
> of Independence, too;
> I hates the glorious Union,
> 'Tis dripping with our blood;
> And I hates the striped banner—
> I fit it all I could.[10]

For the latter James G. Blaine was an eloquent spokesman, even as late as the end of Reconstruction. When a blanket amnesty bill was proposed in Congress in January 1876, Blaine seized on the occasion to uncover old scars and to rekindle the fires of old emotions:

In my amendment I have excepted Jefferson Davis from amnesty. I do not place his exclusion on the ground that Mr. Davis was, . . . the head and front of the Rebellion. . . . But I except him on this ground: that he was the author, knowingly, deliberately, guiltily, and wilfully, of the gigantic murders and crimes at Andersonville. . . .

The poor victim Wirz deserved his death for brutal treatment of many victims; but it was a weak policy on the part of our government to allow Jefferson Davis to go at large and hang Wirz. . . . his execution seemed like skipping over the president, superintendent, and board of directors in the case of a great railroad accident and hanging the brakeman of the rear car.[11]

Blaine was answered by Democratic Congressman Ben Hill of Georgia, a spokesman both of sectional reconciliation and southern states' rights. Neither adversary had been a combat veteran. Blaine served in the U.S. Congress during the war, Hill served as senator in the Confederate Congress.[12] His argument was both pragmatic and emotional:

We had well hoped that the country had suffered long enough from feuds, from strife, and from inflamed passions, and we came here, sir, with a patriotic purpose to remember nothing but the country and the whole country, and, turning our backs upon all the horrors of the past, to look with all earnestness to find glories for the future. . . .

The charge is that he [Jefferson Davis] is a murderer, and a deliberate, willful, guilty, scheming murderer of "thousands of our fellow citizens." . . . [The charge] is nothing . . . but a report of a committee of this Congress, made when passions were at their height. . . .

To you, gentlemen, who seek still to continue strife, and who, not satisfied with the sufferings already endured, the blood already shed, the waste already committed, insist that we shall be treated as criminals and oppressed as victims, only because we defended our convictions—to you we make no concessions. . . . Martyrs owe no apologies to tyrants.

We ask you, gentlemen of the Republican party, to rise above all your animosities. . . . Let us unite to repair the evils that distract and oppress the country. Let us turn our backs upon the past, and let it be said in the future that he shall be the greatest patriot, the truest patriot, the noblest patriot, who shall do most to repair the wrong of the past and promote the glories of the future.[13]

VI *The New South*

According to Ben Hill "There was a South of slavery and secession—that South is dead. There is a South of union and freedom—that South, thank God, is living, breathing, growing every hour."[14]

After four years of bitter fighting the war was over; Hill advocated sectional reconciliation. He would be joined by other southern voices who envisaged rebuilding "their shattered society within the framework of a broad nationalism."[15]

The theme, the New South, found its strongest advocate in Henry W. Grady, the editor of the *Atlanta Constitution*. Though the son of a Confederate officer killed in combat, he was among the first to support nationalism in the South, and yet at the same time to cling to cherished southern traditions, particularly the concept of noblesse oblige and the inferior position of the black. Because of a series of editorials in favor of reconciliation, in 1886 the New England Society of New York asked him to speak at a banquet at Delmonico's.[16]

In his speech he first had words of praise for President Lincoln. Then he described the "footsore Confederate soldier . . . ragged, half-starved" coming home to put in a crop "and fields that ran red with human blood in April were green with the harvest in June." "There was little bitterness" as "cheerfulness and frankness prevailed."[17] And what is the sum of our work he asked:

We have found out that in the summing up the free negro counts more than he did as a slave. We have planted the school house on the hilltop and made it free to white and black. We have sowed towns and cities in the place of theories and put business above politics. We have challenged your spinners in Massachusetts and your iron-makers in Pennsylvania. We have learned that the $400,000,000 annually received from our cotton crop will make us rich when the supplies that make it are home-raised. We have learned that one northern immigrant is worth fifty foreigners; and have . . . wiped out the place where Mason and Dixon's line used to be and hung out latchstring to you and yours. [pp. 87–88]

In conclusion he asked the New Englanders if they would "permit the prejudice of war to remain in the hearts of the conquerors, when it has died in the hearts of the conquered" (p. 92). Here was truly a southerner that said the right things to the Yankees. Here was a warm welcome South for the northern investor.

At the Texas State Fair at Dallas, 26 October 1887 Grady philosophized concerning the role of the black in the New South. What emerged was a potpourri of noblesse oblige, white supremacy, and the myth of black Reconstruction (pp. 94–120):

I want no better friend than the black boy who was raised by my side, and who is now trudging patiently with downcast eyes and shambling figure through his lowly way in life. I want no sweeter music than the crooning of my old 'mammy,' . . . when she held me in her loving arms, and bending her old black face above me stole the cares from my brain, and led me smiling into sleep. I want no truer soul than . . . the trusty slave, who for four years while my father fought with the armies that barred his freedom, slept every night at my mother's chamber door . . . ready to lay down his humble life on her threshold. [p. 97]

After the war there was a problem of the vote. "Into hands still trembling from the blow that broke the shackles, was thrust the ballot." Next, Grady asserted, the blacks were in charge of twelve ex-Confederate states (p. 98). This statement was made despite the fact that only in South Carolina were the blacks in the majority in a southern legislature and no elected governor was ever black:

In less than twelve months from the day he walked down the furrow a slave, the negro dictated in legislative halls from which Davis and Calhoun had gone forth, the policy of twelve commonwealths. When his late master protested against his misrule, the federal drum beat rolled around his strong-holds, and from a hedge of federal bayonets he grinned in good-natured insolence. . . . Simple, credulous, impulsive— . . . is he a safer, more intelligent citizen now than then? [p. 98]

Should the white vote divide, the blacks would hold the balance of power. Thus with their "shiftless habit and irresolution," they "would be forever in alliance with that faction which was most desperate and unscrupulous" (p. 99). That this behavior could be adopted by Grady's "mammy," the black boy raised by his side, and the slave who protected his family during the war, Grady fails to explain.

Two years earlier the Atlanta editor took both strong exception and offense to a different interpretation of the role of the black. Whereas Grady emphasized noblesse oblige, the racial inferiority of the black, and accommodation, fellow southerner George Washington Cable advocated primarily the reformation of the southern white conservative. Cable, a Confederate veteran, and a writer of some reknown, saw the solution to be full citizenship for the blacks. He pointed out in the *Century* magazine of January 1885 that the ex-slaves had "within two decades risen from slavery to freedom, from freedom to citizenship, passed on into political ascendancy, and fallen again from that eminence":[18]

He maintained that the days of noblesse oblige were gone: The abandonment of this relationship was not one-sided; the slave, even before the master, renounced it. Countless times, since reconstruction began, the master has tried . . . to play on that old sentiment. But he found it a harp without strings. The freedman . . . could see, all our old ideas of autocracy and subserviency, of master and menial, of an arbitrarily fixed class to guide and rule, and another to be guided and ruled. He rejected the overture. [p. 412]

Cable then defined the limits of the freedom of the southern black: "In these days of voluntary reconstruction he is virtually freed by the consent of his master, but the master retaining the exclusive right to define the bounds of his freedom" (p. 412). Instead there should be only one class of citizens:

There are those among us who see that America has no room for a state of society which makes its lower classes harmless by abridging their liberties, or, as one of the favored class lately said to me, has "got 'em so they don't give no trouble." There is a growing number who see that the one thing we cannot afford to tolerate at large is a class of people less than citizens; and that every interest in the land demands that the freedman be free to become in all things, as far as his own personal gifts will lift and sustain him, the same sort of American citizen he would be if, with the same intellectual and moral caliber, he were white. [p. 413]

Cable's article was greeted by an avalanche of letters taking issue with his position. To present this view *Century's* editors selected Grady. His answer is indicative of "enlightened" white southern thinking of the day.[19] Grady first pinned the Yankee label on Cable, because of his having northern parents. Thus Cable did not speak for the South. The Atlanta editor found the Louisianian "sentimental rather than practical."[20] The South would never agree with Cable's line of thought—integration. "Neither race wants it" (p. 910). Furthermore, the whites, at any cost and at any hazard, would maintain the clear integrity and dominance of the Anglo-Saxon blood.

Grady strongly supported segregation of public transportation, quoting the separate but equal provisions of state laws (pp. 914–15). Not only in riding but "the white and black races in the South must walk apart" (p. 912). The concept of noblesse oblige was emphasized with the statement that nearly one million black children shared the school taxes equally with the whites, though the whites paid nineteen twentieths of the tax (p. 912). No mention was made of the plight of the sharecropper whose physical labor created much of the tax money.

Grady argued that white southerners had no intention to stifle criticism or avoid issues (p. 917). Significantly, however, he does not mention the problem of the 211 lynchings during the previous year,[21] none of which was punished.

Finally, Grady argued for leaving the problem of race relations to the South. He recognized that the blacks were there to stay. Southern prosperity would be measured by justice to the blacks. The South said:

not boldly, but conscious of the honesty and the wisdom of her convictions:
"Leave this problem to my working out. I will solve it in calmness and deliberation, without passion or prejudice. . . . Judge me rigidly, but judge me by my works."[22]

In answering Grady in the September issue of *Century*, Cable maintained that newspapers and politicians did not represent a silent intelligent majority of southerners. The latter would "act fairly and justly if given the chance."[23] He accused Grady of simplifying civil rights into "social intermingling" (p. 181). Many white people believed incorrectly that civil rights meant social equality. It did not.[24]

Class rule to Cable was un-American. He disagreed with Grady's statement that neither race wanted civil rights for the blacks. The blacks had been praying for twenty years for them: ". . . no party dare say that in these United States there is any room for any one class of citizens to fasten arbitrarily upon any other class of citizens *a civil status* from which no merit of intelligence, virtue, or possessions can earn an extrication" (p. 57). He asked ". . . is every colored man inferior to every white man in character, intelligence, and property?" (p. 81). Grady, who claimed to speak for the South, did not ". . . signify anything better than the right of the white man to rule the black without his consent and without any further discrimination between intelligence and unintelligence or between responsibility and irresponsibility" (p. 84).

VII *Douglass on the Southern Racial Problem*

Throughout most of the nineteenth century Frederick Douglass was the undisputed leader of America's blacks. His last appeal for justice for the blacks was an article in the *A.M.E. Church Review* shortly before his death in February 1895. Douglass asserted that while both northern and southern white men had offered their views on the "Negro Problem," there remained "a perfect epidemic of mob law and persecution now prevailing at the South. . . ."[25] The attitude of the better class of southerners was ominous:

. . . we should be shocked and astonished, not only by these mobocratic crimes, but by the attitude of the better classes of the Southern people and their law-makers, towards the perpetrators of them. With a few noble exceptions, . . . the upper classes of the South seem to be in full sympathy with the mob and its deeds. . . . Press, platform and pulpit are generally either silent or they openly apologise for the mob and its deeds. The mobocratic murderers are not only permitted to go free, untried and unpunished, but are lauded and applauded as honourable men and good citizens, the high-minded guardians of Southern virtue. [p. 4]

Douglass did not defend criminals: "'Let no guilty man escape.' But . . . let no guilty man be condemned and killed by the mob . . ." (p. 7). The veteran black leader denounced the disfranchisement of the Negroes in the South. He mentioned the exemplary behavior of the slaves during the Civil War while their owners were away in the Confederate army (pp. 9–10). He recalled the murder of many blacks in the early days of Reconstruction (p. 12).

He denied that rape was a "special and peculiar crime of the coloured people of the South" (p. 8). He regarded the charge to be a fraud caused by

... a fixed determination to degrade the Negro by judicial decisions, by legislative enactments, by repealing all laws for the protection of the ballot, by drawing the colour line in all railroad cars and stations and in all other public places in the South, thus to pave the way to a final consummation which is nothing less than the Negro's entire disenfranchisement as an American citizen. . . . It is a part of a well-devised reactionary movement against the Negro as a citizen. The old master class are wise in their day and generation. [pp. 15–16]

The Republican party had abandoned its early high principles and had been "converted into a party of money, rather than a party of humanity and justice" (p. 24). Anticipating *Plessy* v. *Ferguson*, he saw the Supreme Court surrendering to the South. The rule of the ex-Confederates was "now nearly complete in many states, and it is gradually capturing the nation's Congress. The cause lost in the war is the cause regained in peace, and the cause gained in war is the cause lost in peace" (p. 24).

"Woe to the South," warned Douglass, "when it no longer has the strong arm of the Negro to till its soil . . ." (p. 28). The landlords of the South once had black labor for nothing. Now they wanted "it for next to nothing" (p. 29). The use of crop lien laws, in addition to forcing the sharecropper to accept his pay in trade at the country store, kept him virtually in peonage (p. 30). To solve the problem Douglass suggested: "Let the white people of the North and South conquer their prejudices. . . . Let the American people cultivate kindness and humanity. . . . Let them [the whites] give up the idea that they can be free while making the Negro a slave. Let them give up the idea that to degrade the coloured man is to elevate the white man. Let them cease putting new wine into old bottles and mending old garments with new cloth" (p. 34).

VIII *Booker T. Washington and The Atlanta Compromise*

Frederick Douglass had been one of the few remaining links tying the Republican party to its antislavery crusade of the antebellum era. Though an ex-slave his power base had been in the North. Now he was to be succeeded as the leader of his race by another former slave who would have his base of operations in Alabama's Black Belt. When the handful of voices of southern black political leaders were being stifled an educator assumed the national black leadership role.[26]

Few figures in United States history have had as controversial a role as Booker T. Washington. At a time when relationships between the two races had deteriorated, when blacks within the Deep South were being disfranchised and segregated, Washington managed to penetrate the power structure, both national and southern, and to obtain not only bargaining power but considerable influence.

His theme at the famous Atlanta Exposition of 18 September 1895 identified him with Henry Grady. To prepare for that moment earlier he had joined in the national capitol a number of prominent southerners to ask for federal funds for the exposition. Small in stature and of unprepossessing appearance, he nevertheless was an impressionable speaker (p. 206). His speech at Atlanta was read first to the Tuskegee faculty for their criticisms (p. 213). Three audiences would be reached at the same time, white northern philanthropists, southern Bourbons, and blacks. His sweeping concession to segregation was the climax of his speech (p. 218).

In all things that are purely social we can be as separate as the fingers, yet one as the hand in all things essential to mutual progress. . . .

The wisest among my race understand that the agitation of questions of social equality is the extremest folly, and that progress in the enjoyment of all privileges that will come to us must be the result of severe and constant struggle rather than of artificial forcing.[27]

He made a strong argument for white employment of black labor with the theme "Cast down your bucket where you are" (pp. 220). He asked that those southerners who were looking to immigrant labor to reconsider. He reminded them of the loyalty, "fidelity and love . . . in days when to have proved treacherous meant the ruin of your firesides" (pp. 220–21).

Washington's address received a generally enthusiastic response. Ex-Governor Rufus Bullock, a prominent Atlanta Bourbon, gave him a symbolic handshake. Editor Clark Howell of the *Atlanta Constitution* had words of praise. The applause from blacks and whites was thunderous. Former abolitionists wrote congratulatory letters. Railroad millionaires Henry Villard and Chauncey M. Depew approved. Letters and editorials demanded that he assume the leadership role formerly held by Frederick Douglass. At the time even W.E.B. DuBois, who would later head the opposition, was enthusiastic.[28]

However, in *The Souls of Black Folk* (1903) which appeared eight years later, DuBois charged that the Atlanta Compromise theme was "the old attitude of adjustment and submission."[29] In an age of more contact among the various races throughout the world, Washington had accepted "the alleged inferiority of the Negro races" (p. 50). Instead of an assertive attitude he preached submission and asked the blacks to give up (1) "political power," (2) "insistence on civil rights," and (3) "higher education of Negro youth, and concentrate all their energies on industrial education, the accumulation of wealth, and the conciliation of the South" (pp. 50–51). After a decade the result of this policy has been (1) "the disfranchisement of the Negro," (2) "the legal creation of a distinct status of civil inferiority for the Negro," and (3) "the steady withdrawal of aid from institutions for the higher training of the Negro" (p. 51).

DuBois then asked if it were possible for blacks to make progress along economic lines if they were "deprived of political rights" and reduced to a servile caste. History, he alleged, answered his question with an "emphatic No" (pp. 51–52).

IX *Summary*

Reconstruction, the first major effort to provide civil rights for the blacks, was doomed to failure for a number of reasons that included the prevalent political thought of the day. Egalitarians, such as Cable, were too few. Southern conservative writers continued to accept the theory of the inferiority of the blacks which earlier proslavery authors had projected. They were supported by northern intellectuals, some of whom were ex-abolitionists, influenced by Charles Darwin and involved in other reforms, illustrated by the activities of the Liberal Republicans and the Mugwumps. These northern intellectuals, while continuing to advocate reform, particularly civil service, accepted the southern thesis concerning the inferiority of the blacks. They failed to see the superficiality of their reasoning.

CHAPTER 7

The Gilded Age

I Introduction

BEFORE the Civil War, the Republicans largely consisted of a loose coalition of old line northern Whigs, former Democrats who were dissatisfied with the southern takeover of their party, idealistic abolitionists, and Know-Nothing remnants with their prejudice against the immigrant and Catholicism. At the center of their ideology was the slogan, "free soil, free labor, and free men." On front stage was the slavery controversy, particularly slavery in the territories. Other major issues included the tariff, internal improvements, homesteads, and banking regulations. Perhaps the most cohesive ingredients of the coalition were emotionalism and the ever present enemy—the South. Despite the inept campaign of John C. Fremont in 1856, the aborted slave-freeing raid of John Brown, and the southern threat of secession, the Republican party, masterfully led by Lincoln, became after 1860 the majority party, a role it would not relinquish until 1932.

II Godkin and the Nation

With the demise of slavery, members of the abolitionist wing of the Republican party shifted their activities to other issues. In line with this new look in the spring of 1865, several former abolitionists banded together with a more moderate antislavery man and planned "a national weekly to perpetuate the hard won goals of freedom and nationality."[1] Its Anglo-Irish editor, E. L. Godkin, was "a doctrinaire laissez faire liberal and utilitarian of the Bentham-Mill school." While superficially supporting the radical cause, he privately opposed Negroes voting (p. 30).

Appropriately, the first issue of the *Nation* celebrated the Fourth of July:

It is not simply the birth of the nation which we now commemorate, but its regeneration; . . . we celebrate not only the close of a long and bloody civil war, but the close of the contest which preceded and led to it, that, . . . "irrepressible conflict" which for half a century absorbed all the intellect of the country, perverted its understanding, corrupted its morals, and employed most of its moral and mental energy, either in the attack or defense, . . . of one of the worst forms of barbarism;—a conflict, too, which, during the last twenty years, began to exercise a paralyzing influence on industry and to poison social intercourse. [2]

The *Nation* predicted great material prosperity after the cessation of hostilities. It also predicted great moral and intellectual and aesthetic results coming from the new wealth. Democracy possessed to a greater degree than other forms of government "the seeds of the highest excellence in every field of culture and research" (p. 5).

For several decades the *Nation*, dominated by Godkin, strongly appealed to intellectuals and the upper middle class. Some of its editorials reflected reform, some were prejudiced, none were dull. Godkin's views on race appear to be a blend of frontier bunkum, Rudyard Kipling, Social Darwinism, together with just plain snobbery: "The dislike of Englishmen and Americans to colored people, and their unwillingness to admit their equality is not due simply to difference of feature, or color, or race, but to difference of feature, color, and race combined with apparent want of mental, moral and physical vigor. People whom an Anglo-Saxon can 'lick' easily he never respects, and cannot readily be got to respect." [3]

His outlook on "The Indian Difficulty" consisted first of attacking the "Indian Ring," the agents, suppliers, and traders. He was aware of the existence of humane people who objected to brutal and cruel treatment of the Indians by the military. He clearly saw the problems of the frontier such as the frontiersman's prejudice against the Indians. [4]

The fact is . . . that the white population comes in contact with the Indians along a frontier line . . . and that the white men along that line are . . . more or less lawless in their habits, quick with their weapons, unscrupulous in their dealings, bitterly prejudiced against the Indians, and but very slenderly influenced by moral or religious ideas.

We are not prepared to deny the Indian the possession of many good qualities; but it cannot be denied, also, that he is a savage . . . and has shown himself, ever since history dawned on him, cruel and treacherous, filthy and dishonest. [p. 544–45]

Godkin's solution for the Indian difficulty was for the Indian to give up his mores and customs, and become a typical middle class white citizen.

On woman's rights Godkin displayed in "A Neglected Side of the Woman's Rights Question," a liberal attitude in favor of granting suffrage:

Nearly all the weapons which are now used against female voting were used twenty years ago to defend the barriers which, in nearly all States, prevented the indiscriminate voting of males, and were all then disposed of. There are no women more ignorant, none more venal, none more selfish than . . . a vast number of men whom the democratic movement of that period admitted to a share in the government. . . . You can no more laugh at female politicians after you have got used to them than at old jokes or twice-told tales.[5]

In politics Godkin particularly objected to the practice of selecting presidential candidates and keeping their participation in the campaign at a minimum:

The great flaw in the working of the governmental machine in our time is the absence of any direct responsibility to the public on the part of the officers, and the absence of any direct means of communication between them. If Presidential candidates had always been expected to justify and commend on the stump the party nomination, there is very little doubt that the practice of nominating obscure and mediocre men and keeping them in strict seclusion till the election, would never have sprung up; and the candidate, on the other hand, would not have been able, as he is now, to protect himself against all responsibility by taking shelter behind the party. . . .[6]

The *Nation*'s longtime editor rejected materialism without humanitarianism. The rise of the shoddy aristocracy was repugnant to him. The robber barons, untrained to the responsibilities of their new power, brought out the aggressiveness in America. The pursuit of profit became the accepted way of life. In his article, "Humanitarianism," Godkin questioned the new morality:

. . . although it is right that charity should cover a multitude of sins, it is in our time allowed to cover too many sins for the good of society; that the growth of law and security and public opinion have, in all civilized countries, removed many of the evils on which the spirit of humanity used in past ages to expend its force, while others peculiar to this age have grown up to which neither the Church nor social nor political reformers can as yet be said to offer any organized or effective resistance. For example—the strong man in our day does not rob on the highway or keep serfs; he thieves in business or on the stock exchange, or swindles the government. . . . We hate slaveholders, aristocrats, rowdies, and all perpetrators of high-handed violence or oppression, but we do not feel unkindly towards an expert speculator or a tricky showman or a fraudulent trustee, if he be a temperance man or an antislavery man or a friend of education, or kind to the poor and the young. The Church and society are both equally indulgent to him.[7]

III   *Social Darwinism*

Although the nation emerged from the Civil War with a southern Democrat as president, radicals Thaddeus Stevens, Charles Sumner, and Ben Wade assumed leadership of Congress following the election in 1866. To insure their dominance, they supported for the presidency in 1868 the war hero, U. S. Grant. Times, however, had changed. During the war, the captains of industry had joined the Republicans, and Grant provided them with a president receptive to their concept of unrestrained exploitation. Political condottieri, with few principles, played the game of spoils politics with a vigor that warmed the hearts of the robber barons.[8] As society became more materialistic, social idealists wondered if the intellectual and emotional enthusiasm for reform of the antebellum days would ever recur.

Just prior to the Civil War Charles Darwin, an English scientist, developed the concept of evolution in regard to animals. In his *Origin of Species* (1859), he accounted for nature's process of natural selection from the lower order of animals to the highest, emphasizing the "survival of the fittest." His fellow countryman, Herbert Spencer, a strong advocate of laissez-faire and utilitarianism, placed at the center of his philosophy the view, which applied to people, came to be known as Social Darwinism. It was held that rugged individualism brought to the top the most fit, while at the same time the weak and incompetent fell to the bottom.[9]

With the appearance of giant industrial complexes, Social Darwinism replaced both the infant industries argument of Mathew Carey and the old philosophy of the classical economists. Rugged individualism, previously held in high esteem on the frontier, became a simple justification for business success. The survival of the fittest brought wealth to the competent, poverty to the weak.[10]

IV   *William G. Sumner*

In America liberals discovered in Spencer's writings justification for the new post-Civil War way of life.[11] A former minister and long time professor of political and social science at Yale, William Graham Sumner became the foremost advocate of Spencerian thought. Sumner projected the existence of cosmic laws that justified the survival of the fittest, competition, and the acquisition of wealth.[12]

Though Sumner advocated Social Darwinism he was not an ardent supporter of several major Republican policies of the Gilded Age. For example, he conducted a valiant fight for free trade.[13] "Protectionism seems to me to deserve only contempt and scorn, satire and ridicule. It is such an arrant piece of economic quackery, and it masquerades under such an affectation of learning and philosophy, that it ought to be treated as other quackeries are treated."[14]

To those who supported high tariffs and also claimed to be ardent capitalists, he answered that "protectionism is socialism. . . . *Socialism is any device or doctrine whose aim is to save individuals from any of the difficulties or hardships of the struggle for existence and the competition of life by the intervention of 'the State.'* Inasmuch as 'the State' never is or can be anything but some other people, socialism is a device for making some people fight the struggle for existence for others" (p. 79).

The Yale professor saw a startling similarity between labor unions and trusts: their viewpoints, however, were different. As products of the nineteenth-century industrial revolution both faced the same problem. If they should combine, they would create a mammoth trust: "The motives of coercion, discipline, and strict internal organization are the same in both cases, and some of the sanctions are the same . . ." (p. 262).

On the growing role of the state, Sumner expressed both concern and opposition. He felt that voters not only lacked the ability to cope with the issues, but shrunk from the responsibility: "We are more inclined to do here what we should do in any other affair—seek for competently trained hands into which to commit the charge. . . . The opinion seems to be gaining ground that, for fear of power, we have eliminated both efficiency and responsibility . . ." (p. 325).

Struggles for power within the country involved various interests seeking larger "shares of the product of industry."[15] Perhaps the solution "would be to leave it to free contract under the ploy of natural laws" (p. 222). If this were not done, and there were continued interference by the government, what would prevent the country from returning to the Middle Ages with its "reiterated and endless interference, with constant diminution of the total product to be divided?" (p. 222).

Sumner warned that while the government was "reaching out on one side to fields of socialistic enterprise, interfering in the interests of parties in the industrial organism, assuming knowledge of economic laws which nobody possesses, taking ground as to dogmatic notions of justice which are absurd, and acting because it does not know what to do, it is losing its power to give peace, order, and security" (p. 224). He maintained "that it is at the present time a matter of patriotism and civic duty to resist the extension of State interference" (p. 225).

Sumner avidly opposed the Spanish-American War, imperialism, and militarism. He defined imperialism as "ruling others without constitutional restraints." He recalled that this occurred in the South during Reconstruction. The right to disagree was trampled on: "We fly into a rage at anybody who dissents and call him 'rebel' and 'traitor,' as strikers shout 'scab' at anyone who chooses to hold an opinion of his own. . . . The evil of imperialism is in its reaction on our own national character and institutions, on our political ideas and creed, on our way of managing our public affairs, on our temper in political discussion" (pp. 346–47).

V *Andrew Carnegie*

Bobbin boy Andrew Carnegie, in a rags to riches saga, created a steel empire. Superb at organization and administration, with extremely limited formal education, Carnegie nevertheless was a prolific writer. Although after 1870 he acknowledged his indebtedness to Spencer, there is no evidence that he either communicated with Sumner or read any of his writings.[16]

His *Triumphant Democracy* (1886) expressed the faith of middle America during the Gilded Age. It explained the similarity between the two major parties, and the identification of the blue collar worker with the middle class. Carnegie also defended nineteenth-century capitalism in terms of the democratic mission of America.[17] The freedom of the New World contrasted favorably with the restrictions of the Old.

Once in four years he [the American] warms up and takes sides, opposing hosts confront each other and a stranger would naturally think that only violence could result whichever side won. The morning after the election his arm is upon his opponent's shoulder and they are chaffing each other. All becomes as calm as a summer sea. He fights "rebels" for four years and as soon as they lay down their arms invites them to his banquets. Not a life is sacrificed to feed his revenge. Jefferson Davis, educated at the National Military Academy and a deserter from the State, is allowed to drag on his weary life in merited oblivion.[18]

The situation in Germany was entirely different: "The German loves his native country, but hates its institutions. Prince Bismarck's yoke is neither light nor easy. Universal military service, the blood-tax of monarchies, is calculated to set the best minds among the bone and sinew to thinking over the political situation, and O, America! how bright and alluring you appear to the down-trodden masses of Europe, with your equal laws, equal privileges and the halo of peace surrounding your brow!"[19]

Carnegie preferred to think that his philanthropic pursuits "were based upon rational, systematic principles."[20] He thought himself to be in the avant-garde of scientific philanthropy. In 1889 he contributed to the *North American Review* a series of articles that later were reprinted in book form as *The Gospel of Wealth*.[21] Here he asserted that the "The gospel of wealth but echoes Christ's words. It calls upon the millionaire to sell all that he hath and give it in the highest and best form to the poor by administering his estate himself for the good of his fellows . . ." (p. 43).

Despite its title, the book is not a religious tract. It is a polemic for the free enterprise system based upon Social Darwinism. Competition is emphasized rather than love: "The price which society pays for the law of competition, like the price it pays for cheap comforts and luxuries, is also great, . . . and while the law may be sometimes hard for the individual, it is best for the race, because it insures the survival of the fittest in every department. We accept and welcome . . . great inequality of environment; the concentration of business, industrial and commercial, in the hands of a few; and the law of competition between these, as being not only beneficial but essential to the future progress of the race" (p. 4).

Stewardship under the Gospel of Wealth involved a moral obliga-
tion of philanthropy for the deserving poor. "The individual administrator of surplus wealth has as his charge the industrious and ambitious" (p. 22). These could be helped by "free libraries, parks, and
means of recreation, by which men are helped in body and mind;
works of art, certain to give pleasure and improve the public taste;
and public institutions of various kinds, which will improve the
general condition of the people . . ." (p. 18).

However, Carnegie had no patience in charity for "the slothful, the
drunken, the unworthy," or the undeserving poor (p. 6). Such expenditures for these people compounded the problem rather than
cured it. To give to a beggar was an extremely selfish act on the part of
the giver, particularly if the money were spent improperly (pp.
16–17).

Carnegie's philosophy of noblesse oblige caught the attention of
William Jewett Tucker, one of the foremost leaders of the liberal
theological "Andover movement." The same year—1891—that
Tucker evaluated the Gospel of Wealth, he had been a leading mover
in establishing the Andover house in South End Boston. This was the
first settlement house in New England and only the fifth in the
United States. Tucker was an activist as well as an ivory-tower
philosopher.[22] After carefully examining Carnegie's gospel in the
Andover Review in June 1891 he credited the steel magnate with
independence, business sagacity, breadth of view, and having a
generous motive. The elitism in Carnegie's philosophy he saw in the
clear bold assumption that wealth was best placed in the hands of a
few.[23] On this he dryly commented that "the inevitable factor in
society is not so certainly the poor as the rich. The rich ye have with
you always" (p. 633). In evaluating Carnegie's thesis, Tucker thought
that the millionaire had misplaced values:

The question is not, How shall private wealth be returned to the public? but,
Why should it exist in such bewildering amounts? Mr. Carnegie's gospel is
really a belated gospel. It comes too late for a social remedy. What it does
accomplish is to call attention to the fact of the enormous surplus of private
wealth, the honest and courageous endeavor of a millionaire to return his
fortune to society, and his call to his fellow-millionaires to do likewise, brings
them, as a class, before the public, and puts the public upon a reckoning of
the volume of wealth in their hands. Consciously or unconsciously, Mr.
Carnegie has hit upon the great object-lesson in our economic civilization. It
is not pauperism, conspicuous and grievous as that is, but the concentration
of wealth. [p. 637]

The basic problem, according to Tucker, was not redistribution but distribution. Tucker would not hinder Carnegie's benevolence but he felt that the concept that wealth was best based in the hands of a few should be challenged (p. 645).

VI　*The Homestead Strike*

The story of the Homestead Strike reveals within Carnegie the contrast between moral humanitarianism and the ruthless struggle for gain.[24] In *Forum* for August 1886 he moralized: "I trust the time has gone by when corporations can hope to work men fifteen or sixteen hours a day. And the time approaches, I hope, when it will be impossible, in this country, to work men twelve hours a day continuously."[25] He also had words of praise for "Messrs. Wihle and Martin, of the Amalgamated Iron and Steel Association," who, he predicted, "will gain and retain power" (p. 145).

Practical business consideration, however, was to have first priority. In 1892 Carnegie and his lieutenants came to the conclusion that wages should be lowered and the union broken at their Homestead, Pennsylvania, plant. The strike was precipitated by Henry C. Frick, in charge of the operation and strongly supported by Carnegie, who rejected union proposals for a new contract.[26]

The *North American Review* that September presented the strike from three viewpoints. Chairman of the congressional investigating committee, Democratic conservative William C. Oates was an ex-Confederate combat veteran from Alabama. Later, with firm support from the Louisiana and Nashville Railroad together with the business and planter elements, he would be elected governor. His observations on the strike show some insight. He pointed out that the protective tariff which destroyed foreign competition did not always benefit the workers. According to Oates, Frick, in employing the Pinkerton detective service rather than appealing to state and local law authorities, made his greatest mistake. Organizations of workers, farmers, and businessmen were legal but no organization had a right to break the law. Oates strongly supported the principle of the open shop:[27] "The right of any man to labor, upon whatever terms he and his employer agree, whether he belongs to a labor organization or not, and the right of a person or corporation (which in law is also a person) to employ any one to labor in a lawful business is secured by the laws of the land" (p. 362).

The southern conservative clearly saw the antiunion feelings of Frick. He felt that had Frick dealt with the workers from the viewpoint of falling steel prices and common sense, the strike would have been avoided (p. 361). Nevertheless, a union could make its members zealots, and unreasonable demands could boomerang. Oates strongly supported the philosophy of laissez faire, particularly insofar as interference by Congress was concerned. Labor troubles were matters for states to settle (pp. 363–64). Congress could make its contribution "by repealing all class legislation and greatly restricting foreign immigration" (p. 364). The key to the solution of labor trouble was states rights: "The legislature of every state should be diligent in enacting wise, conservative and just laws for the protection of both labor and capital, so that demagogues may have a narrower field for agitation" (p. 364). Just how the rights of the laboring men were to be protected, other than by platitudes, Oates did not explain.

Retired constitutional and patent lawyer, George Ticknor Curtis, took the strikers to the woodshed in the second article. Perhaps typical of the conservative intellectual who had led a cloistered existence, Curtis had little sympathy for the problems of the working man. His own background was marked by certain inconsistencies: although during the antebellum era he had defended Dred Scott, he had also strongly supported the fugitive slave law in facilitating the return of an escaped bondsman. Even though, with pacifist leanings, he had opposed Lincoln's call to arms, armed force against the Amalgamated Association of Iron and Steel Workers to him was perfectly legal. The issue at stake at Homestead to Curtis was law and order. Not only were the actions of the Carnegie iron and steel firm legal, but the actions of the labor union lawless and murderous. Indeed, any strike was a crime against the state:[28] "The stake that society has in all branches of manufacturing industries and in all the great lines of communication and travel is too vast to permit any body of men, large or small, on any pretext, to put a sudden stop to production, or to cause a sudden paralysis in the system of daily and hourly intercourse between different communities."[29]

Since Carnegie was a Republican, Curtis accused the Democrats of making the strike a campaign issue. On the other hand, Republican politicians and newspapers attacked the Democratic executive of Pennsylvania for "pusillanimous hesitation" (p. 368). A strong supporter of the open shop principle, Curtis accused those who followed the decisions of a labor union of committing moral suicide. Labor union members should limit themselves to discussion, information, and mutual aid (pp. 369–70).

Completely oblivious to the terrible working and living conditions of many workers caught in a labor market dominated by employers, black lists, yellow dog contracts, and the like, and without any meaningful legal protection, Curtis closed his article by claiming a similarity between labor unions and slavery: "We have emancipated the colored race from slavery; certain portions of our own race need emancipation from a slavery that is just as bad" (p. 370).

A strong dissent to the emphasis on the right of property was tendered in the third article by Terrance V. Powderly, General Master Workman of the Knights of Labor. Although Powderly compared the workers with the patriots of 1776, his argument was more relevant to the Industrial Revolution. Times had changed. Instead of the close employer-employee relationship of the early republic, the typical business enterprise—the corporation—dealt with workers through a superintendent.[30]

The corporation, composed of many men, is an association of capital which delegates its authority to an agent whose duty it is to deal with the workmen and make terms with them. The Amalgamated Association, and all other bodies of organized workmen, stand in the same relation to the men as the corporation does to the capitalists whose money is invested. One invests money, that is, his capital; the other invests his labor. . . . That the workman should have the same right to be heard through his legitimately appointed agent, the officer of the labor organization, that the corporation has to be heard through the superintendent or agent, is but equity. [pp. 371–72]

Powderly credited labor unions for being responsible for every gain that the workers enjoyed. He dismissed the contribution of philanthropists as mere "honeyed words" (p. 372). Insofar as the right of property, he credited the labor of the workers for being responsible for the prosperity of Homestead. He also recalled that the steel interests, in advocating a high tariff and protection for American steel, had used as their chief argument that such laws were in the interest of labor. It was never argued that capital was being protected (p. 373). Instead, "The workman has not been protected from foreign competition by the government. He has had to fight the battle for himself through the labor organization. Not only has he had to fight against foreign competition, largely attracted by our delusive tariff laws, but he has had to wage war with the employer for a share of that protection which his government decreed by law that he should have."[31]

With the federal and state governments now using armed forces and business people—the Pinkertons—to break strikes, Powderly and the Knights of Labor advocated "the enactment of laws, providing for arbitration between employers and employed" (pp. 373–74). The arbitration process was to be followed before a strike or lockout would be resorted to.

Powderly then attacked the evils of the Industrial Revolution: "The system which makes one man a millionaire makes tramps and paupers of thousands. . . . The millionaire becomes more arrogant and unreasonable as his millions accumulate. Victimizing and blacklisting are the concomitants of the rule of industrial establishments by our millionaire 'lords of industry' . . ." (p. 374).

He then quoted from a statement by Carnegie of six years previous:

To expect that one dependent upon his daily wage for the necessaries of life will stand by peaceably and see a new man employed in his stead is to expect much. . . [T]he employer of labor will find it much more to his interest, wherever possible, to allow his works to remain idle and await the result of a dispute than to employ the class of men that can be induced to take the place of other men who have stopped work. . . . There is an unwritten law among the best workmen: "Thou shalt not take thy neighbor's job." No wise employer will lightly lose his old employees. [p. 375]

Powderly concluded his defense of the Homestead strikers by asserting that "what the law will not do for men they must do for themselves, and by the light of the blazing guns at Homestead it was written that arbitration must take the place of 'Pinkertonism'" (p. 375).

VII   *Edward Bellamy*

The son of a Baptist preacher, Edward Bellamy first studied law, then found employment as a journalist, and finally discovered his niche as a novelist.[32] His Odyssey involved a revolt against the Calvinist doctrine of innate depravity. His sensitivity to nature was similar to that of Thoreau's. He lived not one life but several.[33] His biographer, Arthur E. Morgan, claims that in *Looking Backward* "he took Utopia out of the region of hazy dreamland and made it a concrete program for the actual modern world" (p. ix). According to Morgan, like Thomas More in *Utopia*, Bellamy patterned his book after the pre-Spanish Peruvian society (p. xv).

Looking Backward is the story of Julian West, a wealthy Bostonian Rip Van Winkle, who fell asleep in the Gilded Age (1887) and awakened in Utopia (2000). His view of the materialism and lack of humanitarianism of the 1880s established the contrast for his dream:[34] "It was only because the masses worked very hard and lived on short commons that the race did not starve outright, and no considerable improvement in their condition was possible while the world, as a whole, remained so poor. It was not the capitalists . . . but the iron-bound environment of humanity . . ." (p. 17).

Others felt that the country was approaching a "social cataclysm" (p. 18).

Awakening in his Utopia of 2000, West discovered that there are "no parties or politicians, and as for demagoguery and corruption, they are words having only an historical significance" (p. 60). What had happened was that industry and business within the United States had been nationalized, including farming, railroads, factories, and capital. The principle of universal military service became the solution to the labor problem (pp. 61–62).

Gone were rugged individualism, squalor, materialism, political parties, dissent. In their place was a New Harmony, Indiana, that worked. The United States was a giant cooperative with woman's rights, no crime, no evil thoughts, no selfishness. The caste and class system was eliminated. The retirement age was forty-five. Middle age and old age were the enviable times of life in the new benevolent society (pp. 60–61, 154 ff.).

Looking Backward sold over a million copies. It led to the birth of the Nationalism movement that advocated the Bellamy Shangri La. The emergence of the Populist party in 1892 reflected the popularity of Bellamy's thinking.[35]

VIII *Pragmatism*

Perhaps the seeds for the destruction of the acquisitive exploitation of the nation were contained in the rise of a new philosophy which has come to be known as pragmatism. It had as its characteristic doctrine that the meaning of conceptions is to be sought in their practical bearings, that the function of thought is as a guide to action, and that the truth is preeminently to be tested by the practical consequences of belief. Pragmatism, the philosophy of experienced expediency, was first presented as a formal doctrine by Charles S. Peirce around 1878. The term pragmatism was introduced by William James in

1898. Americans have traditionally taken pride in being practical men. Though much of American political theory is of foreign import, the emphasis in this country has been on the practical. Indeed, theory is often looked upon as a function of idle dreams. Workability has ever been the acid test. With William James truth became a variable entity rather than an abstract absolute. The test of truth was in the practical application.[36]

John Dewey, a philosopher and professor at the University of Chicago and later Columbia, developed a variation of pragmatism which he called instrumentalism. Starting with *Psychology* in 1887, in a series of books he pointed pragmatism in the direction of society and made it an instrument for social action. He disregarded natural laws and natural rights along with natural determinism whether of the Spencerian or Marxian variety. He argued that, since man controlled his environment as much as the latter controlled him, there should be continuous experimentation. In Dewey's view of America there was common participation in the tasks and in the enjoying of the fruits of labor.[37] He would influence both the progressives and the rebels of the World War I era.

CHAPTER 8

Populism, Imperialism, and Turn of the Century Politics

I Populism and the Election of 1892

NUMEROUS small farmers, particularly of the South and West, did not share in the postwar boom even though the Industrial Revolution brought the railroads to provide much needed transportation for carrying their crops to market. At the same time they observed their Civil War heroes, now Bourbon railroad and corporation lawyers, in a political and economic alliance with the nouveau riche of the East. Disillusioned, they found themselves contending particularly in wheat and cotton, in a world market both without protection against their competitors and without control over output. Supply outpaced demand in wheat, corn, hogs, and cotton as India, Australia, and Argentina competed with the United States.

Expressing frustration, farmers were told that overproduction accounted for the low prices. Nevertheless, they came to see that a result of the Civil War had been the victory of commerce and industry over agriculture. To regain lost ground, rural people turned first to the Grange which by 1871 was firmly established in the South and West. Its political leader, General James B. Weaver, ran on the Greenback ticket for the presidency in 1880.

Congressman, as well as soldier, Weaver had grown up on the Iowa frontier. As a fourteen-year-old he had delivered mail through roadless country and across bridgeless streams. In the 1850s he had participated in the California gold rush. When the Civil War came, Weaver had been in the thick of combat, taking command of his regiment in the Battle of Corinth. At the end of the war he was brevetted brigadier general. First a Democrat, then a Republican, he became a Greenbacker and was elected to Congress in 1878.[1]

Despite the political activity of the Greenbackers in 1876 and 1880, after 1875 the Grange disintegrated. In the South white farmers would not desert the Democratic standard. Out of Texas in the late 1880s the Farmers Alliance spread through the South and West as the farmers and rural people once again organized to improve their economic well-being. The next step was the formation of the first strong third party since before the Civil War.

While most of its members were still within the two major parties the Farmers' Alliance in 1889 met at St. Louis to plan a merger with the Knights of Labor. The Alliance then the following year gathered at Ocala, Florida, and issued the famed Ocala Demands:

1. We demand the abolition of national banks, and the substitution of legal tender treasury notes in lieu of national bank notes. . . .
2. We demand that Congress shall pass such laws as shall eventually prevent the dealing in futures of all agricultural and mechanical productions. . . .
3. We demand the free and unlimited coinage of silver.
4. We demand the passage of laws prohibiting the alien ownership of land, . . . and that all lands now held by railroads and other corporations in excess of such as are actually used and needed by them be reclaimed by the government and held for actual settlers.
5. Believing in the doctrine of equal rights to all and special privileges to none, we demand that taxation, national or state, shall not be used to build up one interest or class at the expense of another.[2]

The more radical wing of the Farmers' Alliance then bolted from both parties and formed the People's party, better known as the Populists. In the new party were also Knights of Labor, single taxers, women righters, prohibitionists, and the Anti-Monopolists.[3]

Their candidate for president, Old Greenback warhorse, General Weaver, published in late 1892 *A Call to Action*. Weaver's main issue was his indictment of the trusts:

One of the main charges against Charles the First, was that he had fostered and created monopolies. His head went to the block. Nearly every great struggle of the English race has been caused by the unjust exactions of tribute—against the extortions of greed. Our own war for Independence was a war against taxes. Our late internal struggle was for the freedom of labor and the right of the laborer to possess and enjoy his own. That struggle is still on and it is now thundering at our gates with renewed energy. It will not down, though the Trust heap Ossa upon Pelion. The people will rise and overturn the despoilers though they shake the earth by the displacement.

These vast struggles are great teachers and the world is learning rapidly. We are coming to know that great combinations reduce the cost of production and soon the world will grasp the idea that the people can combine and protect themselves. In this combine, in this co-operation of all, there will be no discrimination and the bounties of Heaven will be open alike to the weak and the powerful. We welcome the conflict. There is no time to lose nor can the battle begin too soon.[4]

He also attempted to destroy the national banking system, substituting for it the subtreasury plan. Congressmen, he held, "were quick to appropriate money to remove trivial obstructions in our navigable streams and harbors, but when it comes to removing obstacles which annually throw the whole commerce of the country into confusion, they shrink back aghast and palliate their criminal neglect of duty by denouncing all who clamor for reform" (p. 428).

Weaver boldly attacked the existing political parties, reasoning that "most men make a stagger at business, not knowing exactly what they want even in this, and then transfer all matters pertaining to Government to the charlatans and the bosses. The rightful and proper rulers of the country are generally asleep, and the butler is dispensing the hospitalities of the mansion to the thieves and vagabonds in the pantry" (p. 432).

According to the veteran third party leader, on only one issue was President-elect Cleveland clear. He was in favor of the Civil War. Weaver proposed that the parties should have meaningful platforms. Congress should return to its former place of importance (pp. 433–35). It should control "commerce, money, transportation and telegraphy" (p. 436). An equitable system of landholding should be devised. The Ocala Demands pointed the way to how all this could be accomplished (p. 436).

Another Populist leader, Mary Elizabeth Lease, wrote in *The Problem of Civilization Solved* (1892):

We are ready for a new movement. Let us lay aside our prejudices, and unite in a patriotic effort to raise the masses of mankind in the scale of humanity.

Let us place America at the head of a federated continent. . . . Let us for the time being merge our republicanism, our democracy and populism in the one grand movement of *Americanism*. Our watchword:—Justice for all, and our war cry the Americas for the Americans.

Nationalize the railroads, telegraph and all labor-saving machinery and end the cause of industrial strikes and business disquietudes.

Free trade in federated America and tariff on alien products will solve the problem of the tariff.

Free coinage of American gold and silver, and the issue of treasury notes, *redeemable by taxation*, will settle the financial problem.[5]

According to Mrs. Lease, poverty, militarism, and metallic money served only as reminders "of a barbarous past" (p. 289). A prohibitionist, she saw politics and beer as "kindred souls." Decay had set in: "The patriotism of Webster, Clay and Lincoln has degenerated into a ham sandwich, free lunch, cocktail article, for sale to the highest bidder. An army of deadbeats, corrupt public officials swarm everywhere" (p. 329).

The magic solution was "the initiative and referendum system of voting" that would "banish lobbyists and boodlers and give untrammeled freedom to public opinion" (p. 268).

Tom Watson, a Democratic congressman from Georgia, bolted to support the Populists in 1892. Writing in *Arena*, July 1892, "Why the People's Party Should Elect the Next President," Watson asserted that a Republican victory would perpetuate class rule. A Democratic victory would continue special privileges for corporations and national banks. Further, President Cleveland had repudiated free silver, a key issue with the Populists. Watson accused American millionaires of responsibility for the repeal of the income tax in 1873. In the field of conservation, both parties had squandered the public domain. Further, Democrats and Republicans alike continued to wave the "bloody shirt" and to grant special privileges to railroads.[6]

Unaware of much of America west of the Hudson river and south of the Mason-Dixon line, yet not as cloistered as George Ticknor Curtis, E. L. Godkin was aghast at the antics of the Populists. Perhaps the only type reform acceptable to the eastern Mugwump types was Manchester liberalism and good government remedies (termed "goo-goo's").

Godkin's polemic in the *Nation* of 7 July 1892 indicted the undeserving poor and the Populists. Insofar as Weaver and his record were concerned, Godkin replaced objective critical thinking with extreme prejudice.

The People's party Convention, which has just completed its sessions at Omaha, was the most largely attended and most thoroughly representative national gathering which any third party has ever got together. All sections of the country sent delegates, and the delegates were full of enthusiasm. The dominant tone of the assembly was discontent with existing conditions. A large part of this discontent was the vague dissatisfaction which is always felt by the incompetent and lazy and "shiftless" when they contemplate those who have got on better in the world. But there was also manifested that spirit of doubt as to the tendencies of our social development of late years which is shared by many thoughtful and philosophic observers, and which causes such observers to question whether something should not be done to check these tendencies. Practically the platform declares that everybody could be made happy if the Government would print a vast quantity of paper currency, allow free coinage and foist light-weight silver dollars upon the country, establish an immense loaning agency, and take control of the railroads. In other words, the fundamental theory of the party is that the Federal Government is an institution of such omniscience and omnipotence, such a repository of wealth and wisdom, that it can be trusted with limitless power. In short, the theory holds that a paternal government can make all its children "healthy, wealthy, and wise." General Weaver is the proper candidate for President of such a party. He is a demagogue who came to the surface in the Greenback period, and was nominated for President by that element in 1880. He is the sort of man who is always made to take up with any new organization which can give him either office or prominence, and no platform could be constructed so ridiculous that he would not gladly stand upon it. He is the fit product of a convention in which Ignatius Donnelly was one of the most popular orators.[7]

Even more extreme against radical thought and Populism were the fulminations of the grandson of Mathew Carey, author of *The Olive Branch*. Henry C. Lea, Philadelphia patrician, historian, and publisher, approved of only prim and proper reform. Carey had influenced this young scion of an old Quaker family. Lea's eleventh commandment was the protective tariff and "the amazing progress and prosperity of the country . . . sufficient proof of the wisdom of Republican tariff measures. . . ."[8]

An early advocate of civil service reform, Lea spent his life supporting "good government in city, state, and nation."[9] Ignoring the Populists, he saw the Democrats as a clear and present danger to the nation in 1892.

The Republican Party has honestly proclaimed its views and purposes; it points to its record and asks to be judged by it; its candidate does the same, and no voter can doubt as to its principles and policy. On the other hand, the Democracy is engaged in a gigantic bunko game, with Mr. Cleveland as bunko-steerer in chief. To satisfy the free-trade sentiment of the South and West, and to placate the Alliance, the Chicago platform borrowed a plank from the Montgomery [Confederate] Constitution and declared it "a fundamental principle of the Democratic Party that the Federal Government has no constitutional power to impose and collect tariff duties except for the purpose of revenue only."[10]

Unaware of the tremendous conflict in the South between the Bourbon Democrats and the Alliance people, Lea saw the followers of Cleveland succumbing to inflationist pressures: "Yet the hope of securing Alliance votes in the Southwest by the promise of unlimited supplies of worthless currency was too flattering to be resisted, and the party has irretrievably pledged itself to this suicidal policy . . ." (p. 1472).

Since the Democrats were states' righters, Lea had dire warnings of the drastic economic disaster that would befall in the event of Cleveland's election: "The Louisiana Lottery has already given us ample warning as to the injury which a single State under profligate rule can inflict on her sisters, and should the tax on State currency be removed, we shall see, like a night-growth of mushrooms, thousands of wild-cat banks spring up in remote and inaccessible sections, showering their paper issues on the defenseless community and swindling farmer and laborer, merchant and artisan" (p. 1472).

On different sides of the fence in 1892 insofar as the political campaign, Godkin took his fellow aristocratic Mugwump to task: "Any elementary book of ethics will tell him that to put the worst possible construction on an opponent's language, when an entirely different one is not only possible but far the more probable, and base on it a charge of fraud, is recognized by all moralists as a departure from truthfulness as well as from decency."[11] Instead of supporting reform, Lea was, according to the *Nation*'s editor, urging people to support those who made "a fraudulent and corrupt use of the public service . . ." (p. 312).

The defeat of the Republicans in 1892 was explained in the *Independent*, 24 November, by Bishop Benjamin T. Tanner of the African Methodist Episcopal Church. A northern black, college educated and seminary trained, Tanner was a frequent contributor to leading journals.[12] His tying together the Republican party and the abolitionist movement was farfetched:

Why this Republican "hip and thigh" defeat? . . . The answer is at hand. God called the Republican Party into the world of politics and government as surely as he called the Reformed, the Wesleyan, the Methodist Episcopal and the Congregational bodies into the world of Churches. No more did he speak to Luther and Melanchthon, to the Wesleys, to Asbury and to John Robinson and John Cotton, than did he speak to Garrison, Lundy, to the Lovejoy, Tappans, etc. . . . so from the vocabulary of Liberty was given to these the watchword, Humanity and freedom. So long as this watchword was kept . . . God gave them the victory. . . . Their defeat is plain God does not stand in need of another Democratic Party. . . . If there be a party which has no watchword for Humanity and Freedom, which simply fights for spoils, that party is, and as we have said of right ought to be, the Democratic Party.[13]

By 1894 E. L. Godkin was caustically calling the Republicans Tweedledum and the Democrats Tweedledee. He felt that both parties were giving in to the demand for bimetallism. He opposed "Government meddling with the metallic currency."[14] A return to the past was his solution: "The old-fashioned remedy for abuses or mistakes—turning one party out and putting the other in—is no longer open to the American people. In whatever direction we look, we seem to find both parties advocating the same things" (p. 322).

Accordingly, both parties were satisfied with the continuance of the protective tariff, a heavy income tax, and bimetallism. He saw each too eager to secure votes to do anything about the threat of Coxey's army to property and order (p. 322).

II   *William H. "Coin" Harvey*

Two years after the defeat of the Populists, William H. Harvey published *Coin's Financial School*. Written in terms of questions and answers, it supported "the free coinage of silver at the ratio of 16 to 1."[15] Harvey had a rural border background. With limited education himself, while still in his teens he taught school, becoming a lawyer at the age of nineteen. Between 1884 and 1893 he resided in Colorado, Utah, and California. His book brought him into strong conflict with Chicago conservatives, who disputed his thesis, importing Roswell G. Horr, a New York journalist and lecturer, to debate him.[16] The basis of the debate was "the doctrine set forth in *Coin's Financial School*" (p. 12).

Harvey took the position that deflation reduced the value of property and made it more difficult for debtors to pay their debts.[17] Horr reasoned that money first received its value from the labor that it represented. He criticized the free silver advocates for leaving labor out of the value of money: "Their whole plan seems to be to enable people who have run into debt to pay their debts without returning full value for what they have received, and nowhere do they take into account the much larger army of the human family who live week in and week out on their daily earnings."[18]

Horr failed to mention that one might borrow cheap dollars during inflation—greenbacks during the Civil War—and have to pay his debt in hard money during a deflationary period. The plight of the small farmer and house owner, holding mortgages made in more prosperous times, was ignored. Horr argued that the working people were creditors, expecting pay for the work that they had done in the same sense that a businessman would expect to be paid for his goods and a banker for a loan. Harvey answered that both property and labor were priced in gold rather than also in silver. He also commented on the increase of tenant farmers in New England, New Jersey, and Pennsylvania from 1880 to 1890, leading one to believe that a number of these had lost their farms through foreclosures (pp. 229–30, 244, 247).

III   *Bryan and the Election of 1896*

Soft money had been a third party issue since the appearance of the Greenback party in the presidential campaign of 1876. Finally, at Chicago in 1896 the free silver wing of the Democratic party emerged triumphant.

Elected to Congress in 1890, William Jennings Bryan of Nebraska quickly assumed a leading role in the support of free silver. For this he was singled out by President Cleveland for discipline and stripped of patronage. When Cleveland wrote an open letter to fellow Democrats advocating the continuation of the gold standard, Bryan replied for the free silver side. The Democratic convention in 1896 presented Bryan with a golden (silver?) opportunity.[19]

In his speech to the convention Bryan agreed with Horr's earlier thesis that the wage earner was "as much a businessman as his employer" (p. 85). He denied that bimettalism was a sectional issue. Then in purple prose he completely captivated his audience:

We have petitioned and our petitions have been scorned.
We have entreated, and our entreaties have been disregarded.
We have begged and they have mocked when our calamity came.
We beg no longer. We entreat no more. We petition no more.
We defy them. [p. 86]

The audience then interrupted with a torrent of applause. It was minutes before order could be restored, and the speech resumed. With the Panic of 1893 very much in mind, despite the fact that the national administration was Democratic, he put his party squarely on the side of the downtrodden.

The sympathies of the Democratic party . . . are ever on the side of the struggling masses who have ever been the foundation of the Democratic party. There are two ideas of government. There are those who believe that, if you will only legislate to make the well-to-do prosperous their prosperity will leak through on those below. The Democratic idea, however, has been that if you legislate to make the masses prosperous, their prosperity will find its way up through every class which rests upon them. [p. 87]

Bryan now had his audience completely with him as he concluded his address.

If they dare to come out in the open field and defend the gold standard as a good thing, we will fight them to the uttermost.

Having behind us the producing masses of this nation and the world, supported by the commercial interests, the laboring interests, and the toilers everywhere, we will answer their demand for a gold standard by saying to them: "You will not press down upon the brow of Labor this crown of thorns; you shall not crucify mankind upon a cross of gold." [pp. 87–88]

The convention enthusiastically endorsed Bryan. For the first time since 1860 there was a sharp difference between the Democracts and the Republicans. Fusion with the Populists would further strengthen the Democrats in the South and West. Labor, it was hoped, would provide the swing vote in the East.[20] Andrew D. White, educator and diplomat, likened the Populist-platformed Democrats to the Paris mob that destroyed the Bastille. He feared their coming under the domination of Bryan, Governor John Peter Altgeld of Illinois, and Senator "Pitchfork" Ben Tillman of South Carolina. He accused them of attacking both the Supreme Court, "the best bulwark of the Constitution,"[21] and the civil service reform. The country faced a great crisis (p. 29). It was not to

be settled by men like Governor Waite, with his Jacobin threat of "blood to the bridles of the horses," or Governor Altgeld's concessions to anarchy, or Governor Tillman's sectionalism, or the programme of socialism, or a candidate foreshadowing a deluge of paper money which shall transfer great masses of private property to an oligarchy at Washington; but by strong, thoughtful reasoners, who, not only in the city centres, but in every schoolhouse, and at every cross-roads, shall bring the simplest truths involved home to the hearts and minds of the people.

The question immediately involved is the prosperity and honor of our country. The question remotely involved is the continuance of the Republic. Our greatest encouragement in this crisis is that these questions are to be settled, not as in 1793 by "the red fool-fury of the Seine," but, in 1896, by appeals to reason and patriotism addressed to the sober second thought of the American people. [p. 30]

That White, one of the founders of a great university (Cornell), a strong and intellectual conservative leader, should have such narrow partisan views is disappointing. He completely failed to understand the plight of labor and the farmer. His view of the French Revolution as a blood bath would not be borne out by history. Indeed, his views were a throwback to Federalism and Boston in 1800.

Isaac L. Rice in the same issue of *Forum* in an article entitled "Thou Shalt Not Steal" accused the Democrats of having the qualities of highwaymen. He found their Chicago platform unfairly attacked the federal, state, and city governments, the railroads, the banks, widows and orphans, and business in general.[22] Furthermore, if the Democrats won

> . . . our Government would thereby announce its fraudulent bankruptcy. Simultaneously, our community would lose its ability to pay taxes, all imports suddenly ceasing. . . . The general paralysis of business would . . . cause the stopping of all factories, shutdown all mills, close all avenues of useful employment. Famine . . . would reign throughout the land. . . . Thousands and tens of thousands would perish in the agonies of starvation. . . . In vain would we look for help toward foreign nations. . . . A pirate sailing under the black flag can expect no aid. . . . We cannot be an abomination to the Lord and live. [p. 14]

Few Presidential candidates have been attacked as bitterly as Bryan. A devoutly religious man who had represented a farm belt district in Congress, he became a wild radical in the eyes of such respectable conservatives as Rice and White. Adding to his troubles, although the American Federation of Labor endorsed free silver, its leader, Samuel Gompers, refused to support him.[23]

Although Bryan ran closely in the popular vote, he was decisively defeated in the electoral count. While he would carry twenty-six states, including the solid South, to McKinley's twenty-one states, he would not win in a single state north of the Mason-Dixon line and east of the Mississippi River. It was in the land of Lincoln and in the eastern swing states such as New York, New Jersey, and Connecticut that Bryan lost the election.[24] He failed to get the workingman's vote. To many of them and of the middle class, he was a wide-eyed western radical, a wild man of the prairie.

IV *Imperialism*

The election of 1896 marked the demise of the Populist party, its platform commandeered by the Democrats led by William Jennings Bryan. As the nation approached war over Cuba, imperialism replaced free silver as the prime issue in the country. A young generation was coming to the fore as fewer and fewer Civil War veterans remained active in public life. American business looked for foreign markets, and Captain Alfred Thayer Mahan held forth on the doctrine of sea power. Mahan did not limit himself to a traditional concern for naval warfare. He emphasized the importance of control of the sea lanes in international politics and trade.[25]

In *The Influence of Sea Power upon History, 1660–1783*, he saw sea power as having a profound effect upon the wealth and strength of countries.[26] He lectured at the Naval War College at Newport to that effect. According to his philosophy naval officers were to be more than military men in the narrow sense. Theoretically, their training was not to be neglected, particularly in the geopolitical realm. Mahan's concept of theoretical training for naval officers became the warp and woof of American imperialism (pp. 8–9, 21).

He strongly believed that the national character of Americans fitted the United States to become a great sea power, providing legislative hindrances were removed and the "more remunerative fields of enterprise filled up. . . . The instinct for commerce, bold enterprise in pursuit of gain, and a keen scent for trails that lead to it, all exist; and if there be in the future any fields calling for colonization, it cannot be doubted that Americans will carry to them all their inherited aptitude for self-government and independent growth" (p. 46).

Looking at the position of the United States in terms of world strategy, he listed as critical areas the Panama Canal, the West Coast, the Hawaiian Islands, and China (p. 357). The Boxer Rebellion in China, he viewed as a matter of the gravest urgency. To counteract its detrimental effects, writing in the November 1900 issue of the *North American Review*, he urged concerted action by the European powers, Japan, and the United States. He also emphasized the importance insofar as the Atlantic coast was concerned of the building of an Isthmus canal.[27]

If Mahan was the strategist of the imperialists, then Albert J. Beveridge was their orator. Both were to have a profound effect upon American foreign policy. America was industrializing and expanding. Yet with all the new middle-class prosperity, there was bitter farm discontent and violent strikes. The traditional values of individualism, self-reliance, and Manifest Destiny were being challenged.[28] The Populists failed in their efforts to reshape the country. The fight was now taken over by the progressives.

Both a lawyer and politician, Beveridge was one of these progressives. Typical of many of the young people who grew up in the aftermath of the Civil War, he romanticized armed conflict. Thus it was easy for him to be a strong advocate of imperialism. The Spanish-American War became a holy crusade and the Americans the chosen people of God.[29] Speaking to the Union League of Philadelphia in 1899, he majestically announced: "The Republic never retreats. Why should it retreat? The Republic is the highest form of civilization, and civilization must advance. The Republic's young men are the most virile and unwasted of the world and they pant for enterprise worthy of their power. The Republic's preparation has been the self-discipline of a century, and that preparedness has found its task."[30]

Caught up in white racism, Social Darwinism, and a healthy dose of political ambition, Beveridge displayed a newfound expertise on the Philippines, helped by a trip to the islands in 1899. America's Christian duty was to tame the savages.[31] The Filipino patriot, Aguinaldo, was but a "spoiled child and the Filipinos savage barbarous people."[32] To deliver the islands to Aguinaldo

and his crew would be to establish an autocracy of barbarism. It would be to license spoliation. It would be to plant the republic of piracy, for such a government could not prevent that crime in piracy's natural home. It would be to make war certain among the powers of earth, who would dispute with arms each other's possession of a Pacific empire from which that ocean can be ruled. . . . The blood already spilled was poured out upon the altar of the world's regeneration. . . . Retreat from the Philippines on any pretext would be the master cowardice of history. It would be the betrayal of a trust as sacred as humanity. It would be a crime against Christian civilization, and would mark the beginning of the decadence of our race. And so, thank God, the Republic never retreats. [pp. 15–16]

Four years before Beveridge spoke to the Union League of Philadelphia, Edward Atkinson, an industrialist and economist, attacked imperialism and jingoism in the *North American Review*. Atkinson warned that "the jingo element can only become dangerous through the negligence of the mass of thinking men."[33] He opposed large expenditures for the construction of a new navy. He particularly objected to "Commerce Destroyers," stating that to build two of this class cost a "sum . . . nearly as great as the endowment of our oldest University, Harvard."[34] He labeled their function piratical, and he called upon the English speaking people to outlaw the seizure of private property on the high seas (p. 557). Insofar as annexation of Hawaii was concerned, Atkinson was opposed. The solution was the neutralization of the islands (p. 559).

As a result of the war with Spain, the foreign policy of the United States underwent drastic and far-reaching changes. Horace N. Fisher, in the *Atlantic Monthly*, October 1898, expressed the view that since we had destroyed the colonial empire of Spain, it was our responsibility to preserve peace and order in the Philippines and the West Indies. Fisher interpreted the prewar foreign policy to be based on Washington's Farewell Address.[35] This contained two principles, affirmed by the Monroe Doctrine: "no political entanglements of the United States in European political broils, and an American system apart and separate from that of Europe" (p. 555).

Fisher noted the recent land grabbing in Africa by the European powers. He also observed that China was being partitioned. The cause was the same: "a scramble for foreign markets, with political dominion thrown in to assure their permanence" (p. 558).

He foresaw that the Philippines would become a foreign market for the United States comparable with Japan. Foreign markets were "an absolute necessity not only for industrial prosperity, but for mitigating the conflict between labor and capital" (p. 558). If another country annexed the Philippines, this would upset the balance of power in the Far East. Then, too, Fisher compared favorably the development of the separate states of the United States with the colonial bureaucracy of the other great powers.

When we look back upon the bureaucratic methods adopted by the continental Powers in colonization, and see how little of genuine civilization has accrued to their colonies; when we compare this meagre exhibit with the steady and noble progress of every Anglo-Saxon state, territory, colony and dependency—whether Caucasian or of lower race—in all that makes man happy, prosperous, and progressive, the victory at Manila does seem as an awakening of the Philippines, and such an awakening as may hasten the spread throughout eastern Asia of the blessings of modern civilization. [p. 559]

The theme of the United States was "peace, law, and equity" with no military caste dominating and equal protection under the law. Public education served to uplift the poor and unfortunate, "making them good citizens,—self-respecting and intelligent, and able to take a constantly increasing part in the affairs of government" (p. 559). That one as well versed in history and foreign policy could have such a naive view of domestic affairs is amazing. Fisher closed his article with high praise for the Anglo-Saxon:

The Anglo-Saxon of to-day is the product of a thousand years of continuous effort to make brave and honest men. For centuries we have practiced the art of self-government, until to govern has become an instinct, and to be self-governed a habit. To us power means opportunity to help others; it also means responsibility, not to man only, but to God, for the wise use of the power thus given us. And for this reason we are especially fitted to act as trustees and guardians of inferior races, and peculiarly qualified to fit them eventually to govern themselves. That this is very truth, compare India and Egypt to-day with what they were before the advent of their Anglo-Saxon rulers. [p. 559]

Veteran Democratic politician and secretary of state under Cleveland, Richard Olney, saw the chief characteristic of American foreign relations before the Spanish-American War to be that of isolation. This had two major causes: the Monroe Doctrine and the protective tariff. Olney blamed this policy for "the decay of our navy and the ruin of our merchant marine." He also felt that it induced "an illiberal and unintelligent attitude towards foreigners."[36] Olney stated that at the time of the Spanish-American War "the American people were fast opening their eyes to the fact that they were one of the foremost Powers of the earth and should play a commensurately great part in its affairs" (p. 290). Cuba should now become part of the United States. It has always been treated as vital to our security: "But why do we find ourselves laboring under the huge incubus of the Philippines? . . . If not bound to buy the Philippines by any considerations of honor and duty, was it our interest to buy them?" (pp. 291, 293).

Olney foresaw that possession of the Philippines would be "a source of weakness rather than of strength" (p. 296). A strong naval base would have been much better, protected by an enlarged navy:

We are become an Asiatic Empire . . . environed by all the rivalries, jealousies, embarrasments, and perils attaching to every Power now struggling for commercial and political supremacy in the East, . . . with all our energies and resources, which have proved as more than adequate to the good government and civilization of the white and black races of North America, pledged and mortgaged for the like services to be rendered by us to seven or eight millions of the brown men of the tropics. [p. 296]

Olney predicted that the new international position of the United States would increase the importance of foreign affairs. It would require "a larger Knowledge of the earth and its diverse people; a familiarity with problems world-wide in their bearings; the abatement of racial prejudices; in short, such enlarged mental and moral vision as is ascribed to the Roman citizen in the memorable saying that, being a man, nothing human was foreign to him" (p. 301).

Those with old antislavery idealistic leanings, who had viewed the Civil War as a crusade for individual freedom, found support for letting the Philippines go free in William Vaugh Moody's *Ode in Time of Hesitation*. Moody had a trust in the ultimate victory of the nation's noble spirit:[37]

> Lies! lies! It cannot be! The wars we wage
> Are noble, and our battles still are won
> By justice for us, ere we lift the gage.
> We have not sold our loftiest heritage.
> The proud republic hath not stooped to cheat
> And scramble in the market-place of war;
> . . . .
> Tempt not our weakness, our cupidity!
> For save we let the island men go free,
> Those baffled and dislaureled ghosts
> Will curse us from the lamentable coasts
> Where walk the frustrate dead.
> . . . .
> O ye who lead,
> Take heed!
> Blindness we may forgive, but baseness
> we will smite.[38]

V Turn of the Century Politics

The political situation in the United States in 1900 was reviewed in an article appearing in the *Atlantic Monthly*, in the March and April issues, by Henry Loomis Nelson. Columbia law school graduate and a veteran journalist, Nelson had served as secretary to Speaker of the House John G. Carlisle, a Democrat. He also had been editor of both the *Boston Post* and *Harper's Weekly*.[39]

Nelson recalled that the Republican party after the Civil War became a firm supporter of protection, while the Democrats generally advocated a lower tariff. He also saw the protectionists in both parties committed to the theory that the "government exists for the purpose of creating and maintaining commercial prosperity."[40] It was against these interests within the Democratic party that the revolt in 1896 took place. Nelson characterized the protectionist theory as essentially socialistic. He also felt that the old doctrine of state sovereignty ended with the Civil War. Democratic opposition to internal improvements was abandoned with the need in the South for navigable rivers. The debate on black rights and the southern question now had little substance and was largely political rhetoric (p. 310).

With both parties taking similar positions the rise of the Greenback party in 1876 was caused by "hard times, low prices, scarcity of employment, drastic industrial and social conditions, [which] operated to intensify the feeling against wealth and capital which had been shown for several years by the poor and discontented. . . . These all believed that they were the victims of the 'money power' which was intrenched in both of the old parties" (pp. 316–17).

Western people demanded relief from high tariffs and deflation. They used free silver as a club against the "money power." After 1886, various discontented factions began to unite: first the United Labor party and then the Populists (pp. 317–19). In 1896 they succeeded in gaining control of the Democratic party, demanding "free coinage of silver, government loans on farm produce, government currency to the amount of fifty dollars per capita, government ownership of railroads, telegraphs, telephones, gasworks, and electric plants . . ." (p. 321).

They also advocated changing to a parliamentary-type national government (p. 321).

In the forthcoming campaign, according to Nelson, both the Democrats and Republicans were "dominated by socialistic tendencies," and "from the socialism of protection" had "resulted the socialism of the transformed democracy."[41] The farmers, workers, and quasi-socialists were at war with the plutocracy. They felt that the owners of wealth were oppressing them. As a result of the Spanish-American War, a new issue had emerged, imperialism (pp. 560–61). The Republicans generally favored imperialism, along with the protectionist Democrats and the youth of the country, "whose imaginations have been stirred by the achievements of battles" (pp. 563–64).

Nelson predicted that the Democrats could attract much of the independent vote if they abandoned free silver and Bryan. He mentioned specifically that the gold Democrats, whose defection gave McKinley his victory in 1892, were strongly anti-imperialist. He also thought that they would be joined on that issue by the old Republicans who had opposed slavery (pp. 562, 565). The Democrats would attack the War of the Philippine Insurrection as "cruel and unjust" (p. 567). The money question put the Republicans in a strong position.

However, if the Democratic party abandoned its Populist platform of 1896 and made the issue one "of our occupation of the Phillipines, raising the question of their permanent retention, convincing the people that the Republican party intends to discard the Constitution in governing the new territories, and declaring expressly against the increase of expenditures, commercialism, and militarism, the chances would be in its favor . . ." (p. 568).

CHAPTER 9

Progressivism and the Muckrakers

I Introduction

THE basic problems in political thinking in the earliest part of the twentieth century appeared to be industrialism, urbanism, and the cultural changes brought about by the rise of corporations. For John Dewey the machine, per se, played the role of a tool that could be used either positively or negatively. Others saw the new times differently. Young intellectuals, who had been out of touch with power, rejected materialism. Progressivism appeared to them to be a practical way of reforming the country. However, it had the head of Janus. For older middle-class progressives the main objective was a return to the past, particularly the free enterprise system of the preindustrial era. For younger progressives the goal was order so as to eliminate cutthroat competition and for this controls and stability were needed.[1]

The untamed forces, those which had almost reduced the American dream to a mockery, had their last great political victory in 1900. For decades the voices of protest, Mugwumps, Populists, Independents, church people, labor union leaders, utopian novelists, and settlement-house workers had been increasingly heard. With the assassination of McKinley in 1901 the old order finally passed. President Theodore Roosevelt, rancher, imperialist, rough rider, and political reformer was now president.

Greatly influenced by the Social Gospel movement, progressivism sought to substitute morality for materialism. Cities had grown fantastically; so had their slums. Filth, disease, polluted water supplies, and rickety tenements caused increasing concern. The flagrant disregard for public good by the trusts and the corrupt politics of city machines eventually caused a strong reaction.

Edward Alsworth Ross, professor of sociology at the University of Wisconsin, aptly described in *Sin and Society* (1907) the changes wrought by the Industrial Revolution:

Nowadays the water main is my well, the trolley car my carriage, the banker's safe my old stocking, the policeman's billy my fist. My own eyes and nose and judgment defer to the inspector of food, or drugs, or gas, or factories, or tenements, or insurance companies. I rely upon others to look after my drains, invest my savings, nurse my sick, and teach my children. I let the meat trust butcher my pig, the oil trust mould my candles, the sugar trust boil my sorghum, the coal trust chop my wood, the barb wire company split my rails.[2]

Several reform-minded writers dealt vigourously on the problems caused by a changing America. These included Thorstein Veblen, Herbert Croly, Walter Weyl, and Arthur F. Bentley.

II *Thorstein Veblen*

A withdrawn and contentious college professor throughout his maturity, Veblen, as an immigrant's son in a rural area, was from the beginning an outsider. As a rural boy in the days of Populism it was only logical that he would view business as predatory. In his first book, *The Theory of the Leisure Class* (1899), he looked upon the ruthless materialism of the age and saw change rather than progress. He accused the captains of industry of both making a fetish of leisure and of having as their major objective profit rather than production. Their walking canes became swagger sticks. Conversely, the industrial engineer had as his objective increased industrial skill.

Veblen combined Marxist materialism with pragmatic relativism. He saw man as a creature of history rather than as a rational entity. He not only rejected the myths of America, but he made no commitment to the past, present, or future. To him man had always been a prisoner of his environment. This meant that in the United States of his day the majority of people were prisoners of the captains of industry. Veblen's role was that of an iconoclast rather than builder, diagnostician rather than healer. With tart phrases he indicted capitalism, yet he was critical of Communism. His insistence that technology was the creation of all the people undercut the moral position of corporate ownership. His theory that peace required the abolition of the price system amounted to equating socialism with the survival of civilization.[3] Veblen's laborious style of writing meant that he mostly influenced intellectuals rather than either the middle class or those in seats of power.

III   *Herbert Croly*

If progressivism has a manual it is Herbert Croly's *The Promise of American Life* (1909). Born in New York City, Croly had his philosophy shaped by a number of influences. First, his parents, natives of England, were followers of Auguste Comte, the French philosopher. Second, at Harvard Croly revolted against both his parents and the positivism of Comte. Third, among the college professors who had a strong effect upon him were three philosophers: Josiah Royce, who looked on individuals as integral parts of society; George Santayana, an elitist; and the pragmatist William James.

Croly's thesis was that the federal government had to be strengthened through legislation in order to protect both the small business people and the blue collar workers. Labor unions and large corporations were to be prevented from abusing power. Croly's turning away from Jeffersonian concepts to those of Hamilton called both for a new definition of progress and of liberalism. To return to Jefferson would have been to abandon the industrialization of the nation. America, he held, was no longer isolated. Though conservatives defended the status quo, basing their position largely on Jeffersonian policies and earlier liberal doctrine, Croly saw the need for conscious reform buttressed by nationalism. This reform would refurbish both ideals and institutions. The frontier and the rugged individual of the past were to be replaced by an instrumental state run by experts. That Croly was not an egalitarian was made plain by his view on the inferiority of blacks who, according to him, had moral and intellectual qualities below that of whites. In the fall of 1914, supported by wealthy patrons, Croly established the *New Republic*. It was to be a bridge connecting some of the older progressives with the Greenwich Village radicals.[4]

IV   *Walter Weyl and Arthur F. Bentley*

Somewhat similar to Croly, in the *New Democracy* (1912) Walter Weyl noted the rise of collectivistic thought in the Progressive era. He also saw the abandonment of the individualism of Jefferson and Jackson. No longer was the concept of the least government adequate. Though he admitted that the poor were exploited, he rejected the class struggle thesis of the Marxists. His socialistic solution included government ownership and operation of basic industries. At the same time he advocated more direct democracy including the initiative, referendum, and recall.[5]

Several years earlier Arthur F. Bentley, a pioneer in contemporary behavioral science, utilized quantitative and empirical methods in an important and controversial study, *The Process of Government* (1908). Bentley's analysis of political parties, group pressures and public opinion led him to the conclusion that conflict among groups is at the heart of political action. Twenty years would pass before political scientists would recognize the major impact of Bentley's thesis.[6]

V *Forerunners of the Muckrakers*

In 1889 Jane Addams founded the Hull House in Chicago. A reformer in several areas, she was particularly successful in involving the foreign born in civil affairs. She also played a decisive role in the crusades for woman suffrage and peace.[7]

Addams early saw that private charity was not sufficient to ameliorate successfully all the problems of the disadvantaged: "One of the first lessons we learned at Hull-House was that private beneficence is totally inadequate to deal with the vast numbers of the city's disinherited. We also quickly came to realize that there are certain types of wretchedness from which every private philanthropy shrinks and which are cared for only in those wards of the county hospital provided for the wrecks of vicious living or in the city's isolation hospital for smallpox patients."[8]

Garbage disposal and intellectual development went hand-in-hand according to Addams. When garbage collection became a menace to health, she actively provided a solution. Hull House was "above all a place for enthusiasms" for free spirits (pp. 184, 281ff.): "It is this type of mind which is in itself so often obnoxious to the man of conquering business faculty, to whom the practical world of affairs seems so supremely rational that he would never vote to change the type of it even if he could" (p. 184).

Jacob Riis, a Danish-American journalist and social reformer, came to America as a youth in 1870. Becoming a police reporter, he wrote *How the Other Half Lives* (1890) which exposed many of the abuses of lower-class urban life. Riis observed that seventy-five percent of the people of New York City lived in tenements. Rapid transit to the suburbs had failed to provide relief. The cause for slums was "public neglect and private greed."[9] The story of the tenements was a dark one, according to Riis:

In the tenements all the influences make for evil; because they are the hot-beds of the epidemics that carry death to rich and poor alike; the nurseries of pauperism and crime that fill our jails and police courts; that throw off a scum of forty thousand human wrecks to the island asylums and workhouses year by year; that turned out in the last eight years a round half million beggars to prey upon our charities; that maintain a standing army of ten thousand tramps with all that that implies; because, above all, they touch the family life with deadly moral contagion. This is their worst crime, inseparable from the system. That we have to own it the child of our own wrong does not excuse it, even though it gives it claim upon our utmost patience and tenderest charity. [p. 3]

VI *The Muckrakers*

The era of the muckrakers began in 1902. Early in 1903 S. S. McClure editorialized on the subject of law and order:

Capitalists, workingmen, politicians, citizens—all breaking the law, or letting it be broken. Who is left to uphold it? The lawyers? Some of the best lawyers in this country are hired, not to go into court to defend cases, but to advise corporations and business firms how they can get around the law without too great a risk of punishment. The judges? Too many of them so respect the laws that for some "error" or quibble they restore to office and liberty men convicted on evidence overwhelmingly convincing to common sense. The churches? We know of one, an ancient and wealthy establishment, which had to be compelled by a Tammany hold-over health officer to put its tenements in sanitary condition. The colleges? They do not understand.[10]

Subjects covered by the muckrakers included capital, transportation, labor, civil rights, government, food, and liquor. Treatment varied from careful research to sensationalistic journalism. Their name came from an attack on them by President Roosevelt in 1906. Roosevelt compared them to the Man with the Muckrake in Bunyan's *Pilgrim's Progress*. While he would later claim that he was specifically referring to yellow-press journalism, he would pin that label on all journalistic reformers of the Progressive era.[11]

The yellow-press journalism, referred to specifically by Roosevelt, was a series of articles by David Graham Phillips on special interest domination of the United States Senate. Although a graduate of Princeton, Phillips was primarily a Mid-western voice in New York City. A pronounced radical in his social, political, and religious views, he wrote with sincerity and vigor in attacking corruption. Yet his writing tended to lack depth and to cater to the popular taste. [12]

The theme of his series of articles, "Treason of the Senate," was that wealthy senators served primarily selfish economic interests. Later this theme was utilized in Charles A. Beard's *An Economic Interpretation of the Constitution*, causing a revolution in historical writing, by revealing the holdings and backgrounds of the framers of the Constitution.

Phillips indicted the entire membership by asserting that senatorial dignity and courtesy actually meant a disregard "for the honor and dignity of the American people" who "were smugly sacrificed to the Senate's craftily convenient worship of the Mumbo-Jumbo mask and mantle of its own high respectability." [13] He quoted from a statement by Senator Henry Cabot Lodge of Massachusetts, "There is too much tendency to remember the senators and to forget the Senate" (p. 488). Phillips claimed that the senators collectively were guilty of treason. The Senate was the final arbiter of the sharing of prosperity. Treason was a strong word, but the Senate was hostile to the interests of the American people and more dangerous than an invading army:

A man cannot serve two masters. The senators are not elected by the people; they are elected by the "interests." A servant obeys him who can punish and dismiss. Except in extreme and rare and negligible instances, can the people either elect or dismiss a senator? The senator, in the dilemma which the careless ignorance of the people thrusts upon him, chooses to be comfortable, placed and honored, and a traitor to oath and people rather than to be true to his oath and poor and ejected into private life. [p. 485]

Perhaps the best known of the efforts of the muckrakers was *The Jungle* (1906) by Upton Sinclair. A socialist, in addition to being a muckraker, Sinclair would spend a lifetime crusading. For his novel about life at the Chicago stockyards he lived seven weeks in the area observing and interviewing workers, management, saloon-keepers, clergymen, and settlement workers. Although his account was fiction, it contained sufficient facts to cause both investigations and reform of the meat-packing industry. [14] He even accused them of stealing billions of gallons of city water through secret mains. However, the principal theme of his story was diseased meat, caused by greed of the packing industry:

> The people of Chicago saw the government inspectors in Packingtown, and they all took that to mean that they were protected from diseased meat; they did not understand that these hundred and sixty-three inspectors had been appointed at the request of the packers, and that they were paid by the United States government to certify that all the diseased meat was kept in the state. They had no authority beyond that; for the inspection of meat to be sold in the city and state the whole force in Packingtown consisted of three henchmen of the local political machine! And shortly afterward one of these, a physician, made the discovery that the carcasses of steers which had been condemned as tubercular by the government inspectors, and which there-fore contained ptomaines, which are deadly poisons, were left upon an open platform and carted away to be sold in the city. . . .[15]

Sinclair revived the tale of the rotten beef sold to the United States Army during the Spanish-American War:

> There were cattle which had been fed on "whisky-malt," the refuse of the breweries, and had become what the men called "steerly"—which means covered with boils. It was a nasty job killing these, for when you plunged your knife into them they would burst and splash foul-smelling stuff into your face; and when a man's sleeves were smeared with blood, and his hands steeped in it, how was he ever to wipe his face, or to clear his eyes so that he could see? It was stuff such as this that made the "embalmed beef" that had killed several times as many United States soldiers as all the bullets of the Spaniards; only the army beef, besides, was not fresh canned, it was old stuff that had been lying for years in the cellars. [p. 114]

Charles Edward Russell also exposed the political and economic power of the meat packers in "The Greatest Trust in the World," which *Everybody's* carried in 1905: "In the free republic of the United States of America is a power greater than the government, greater than the courts or judges, greater than legislatures, superior to and independent of all authority of state or nation."[16] Russell accused the meat packers of controlling prices and regulating "traffic in a thousand markets." Their industry was "an absolute, iron-clad, in-frangible monopoly" (2). Not only did they fix the price of meat but with their refrigerator cars the price of fruit. In addition to owning factories and stockyards their trust owned "politicians, legislators, and Congressmen":

It defies Wall Street and all that therein is. It terrorizes great railroad corporations long used to terrorizing others. It takes toll from big and little, it gouges millions from railroad companies, and cent pieces from obscure shippers. To-day it is compelling a lordly railroad to dismiss its general manager, to-morrow it is black-listing and ruining some little commission merchant. It is remorseless, tireless, greedy, insatiable, and it plans achievements so much greater than any so far recorded in the history of commerce that the imagination flags in trying to follow its future possibilities.

It fixes, for its own profit, the prices the farmer of the West shall receive for his cattle and hogs, and the prices the butcher of the East shall charge for his meat. [p. 3]

Russell labeled the meat trust "a great criminal organization" (pp. 251–52). He accused it of raising the cost of living of every household. He asked what should be done to remove its influence which was "powerful enough . . . to undermine and destroy the essentials of free government" (p. 252).

Utilizing the *Saturday Evening Post*, meat-packing executive J. Ogden Armour endeavored to answer the stockyard muckrakers. His articles were later printed in book form as *The Packers The Private Car Lines and the People* (1906). Armour claimed that thousands of people visited Chicago's meat-packing plants without seeing the conditions alleged by Sinclair.[17] He felt that prejudice against the packers was "appealed to by the agitator" (p. 165).

One of the most prolific muckrakers, Ray Stannard Baker, was also one of the more diligent. One of his early journalistic assignments as a Chicago reporter was interviewing Jacob Coxey while he was leading his army to Washington. Baker contrasted the affluent crowds at the World's Fair with the ragged cohorts of Coxey. Becoming an expert on industrial problems, he affiliated with *McClure's*. He attacked corruption and oppression, regardless of its origin.[18] In one of his earlier muckraking articles, during the 1902 coal strike, Baker assailed the anthracite coal miners union for violence against miners who continued to work. There were seventeen thousand miners at work during the strike; of these more than seven thousand were old employees of the coal mining companies. The remainder were miners from elsewhere and workers without previous experience in mining. Baker carefully researched the story of the nonstriking miners because "it seems profoundly important that the public should know exactly who these seventeen thousand American workers really were, how they fared, and why they continued to work in spite of so much abuse and even danger. This inquiry may be made without bias, without contravening the rights of labor to organize, or impugning the sincerity of the labor leader, or defending the operator."[19]

In his treatment of the plight of the nonunion miners, Baker particularly utilized oral interviews to show their side. J. R. Gorman, a nonunion engineer who had worked for a mining company for twenty-five years, was told by the president of the local union that he would have no job when the strike ended. Gorman, who carried a weapon for protection, felt that the mine workers union existed only for striking. It had no beneficial or insurance programs (p. 326).

In another article, "The Reign of Lawlessness: Anarchy and Despotism in Colorado," Baker assailed martial law and the conditions at Cripple Creek, Colorado, which brought it about.[20]

Describing the Cripple Creek miners, Baker reported that they were largely educated, native-born, landowners, and altogether respectable citizens. Yet some of them had been arrested without warrants, and habeas corpus proceedings made a mockery by the military. The staff of a newspaper, the *Victor Record*, was similarly treated. A major cause of the martial law appeared to be the strong reaction to the militancy of the Western Federation of Miners headed by Big Bill Haywood. This reaction also led to the formation of citizens' alliances (pp. 44–47).

In summarizing the predicament of the state, Baker indicted its entire population: "the people have broken the law and they are being punished. Not part of the people, but every person in Colorado; not only he who bludgeoned or bribed, but he who, greedily, in the pursuit of his private business, has forgotten his civic duties, who has not . . . *demanded* the election of men who will enforce the law, not union men, nor corporation men, but Americans" (p. 56).

In "Organized Capital Challenges Organized Labor," Baker attempted to place each in its proper perspective. He pointed out the predicament of the small employer caught between the demands of the unions.[21] He also mentioned the hypocrisy of "The Employers' Association and Citizens' Alliance . . . turning from their horror at the abuse of the nonunion man and employing exactly the same methods themselves" (p. 286). At the conclusion of his article Baker suggested some rules for capital and labor (p. 292).

Among particularly disreputable swindles was the bucket-shop operation. The bucket-shop sharks claimed to be legitimate stockbrokers and bankers providing an investment service for storekeepers, workers, and small businessmen. The so-called private telephone wire of the New York firm of Barry and Co. ran from the counterdesk in the trading room to under the edge of a carpet in an adjoining room and ended there. Merrill A. Teague exposed "Bucket-Shop Sharks" in *Everybody's* (June 1906). Teague called them "the meanest most unscrupulous, and most dangerous class of thieves."[22] He severely criticized stock exchanges, postal authorities, and local police for not prohibiting their operations:

> Bucket-shopping should be suppressed, or placed at par with the pool-room and the poker or crap 'joint' before the law of every State in the Union. The bucket-shop keeper should be hunted by police, secret-service and county officers with the same relentlessness which is shown in the chase of the professional card-sharper, the green-goods operator, the bunco-steerer, the confidence man, the pool-room proprietor and manager, the pickpocket, the safe-cracker, and the porch-climber. [p. 735]

From the standpoint of constructive muckraking, Charles Edward Russell in "The Tenements of Trinity Church" in *Everybody's*, July 1908, played a major role in causing an extremely wealthy Protestant Episcopal Church to reform a policy which had a history of one hundred and twenty years.[23] Russell vividly described Trinity's tenements.

> Drunken, disreputable, decayed, topsy-turvy old houses, the homes of thousands of families and the breeding-places for so many children that are to carry on the world's work—who owns these terrible places? Who draws the wretched profit of their existence?
>
> Trinity Church, holder of one of the greatest estates in New York or in the country owns many of them. This is the heart of her possessions: street after street is lined with her properties.[24]

Russell had praise for the benevolent projects of Trinity: "Look at the year-book of the parish. You will see that Trinity maintains trade-schools, parochial schools, Sunday-schools, missions many kinds of philanthropy. It teaches girls to cook and sew and gives military training to boys. Every summer it gives to the children of its Sunday-school an excursion, up the Hudson . . ." (p. 57). Russell further pointed out that although the owners of Trinity were its communicants, the management of the church was "a self-perpetuating body, without responsibility and without supervision" (p. 57).

In "The Daughters of the Poor," *McClure's*, November 1909, George Kibbe Turner revealed the relationship of the white slave trade with Tammany Hall and corrupt organizations in other cities. Turner explained the hold of a political machine on the poor:

"The people love Tammany Hall," said my host [a resident of the Bowery]. "We use them right. When a widow's in trouble, we see she has her hod of coal; when the orphans want a pair of shoes, we give it to them. . . . As he spoke, the other half of the political financing was shown. The procession of the daughters of the East Side [i.e., prostitutes] filed by the open door upstairs with their strange men. It was the slum leader's common transaction. Having wholesaled the bodies of the daughters at good profit, he rebates the widow's hod of coal.[25]

Turner saw the issues in the forthcoming city election involving all the people against Tammany Hall. "For the rich, the great tax rate for wasted and misappropriated money; for the citizen of average means, the inadequate schools, dirty highways, burglaries, and violence upon the public streets." The main issue "for the people of the tenement districts was" shall New York City continue to be the recruiting-ground for the collection for market of young women by politically organized procurers? (p. 61).

VII *Attacks on Muckrakers*

Not to all were the Muckrakers crusaders in white armor. Ellery Sedgwick, distinguished former editor of the prestigious *Atlantic Monthly*, castigated them in "The Man with the Muck Rake" in the *American Magazine* for May 1906.[26] While admitting corruption existed Sedgwick claimed that the times were better "than the world has ever seen before. . . ."[27] A political revival had occurred. Should not its creed be believed: "'Play the game hard, but play it square and make every man that plays it play it square too?'" (p. 111). The muckraking movement had "begun with sincerity of purpose." It had accomplished "magnificent work for the right . . ." (p. 111). But theories have taken over. The "new journalism," which emphasized both socialism and commercialism, had taken over. On the one hand, it was dominated by money and power, on the other, muckraking led to socialism and the destruction "of the government of our forefathers" (p. 112). The typical Muckraker was heaping up "Exaggeration, perversion, distortion, truths, half-truths, lies . . . regardless of honesty, reckless of consequences, absolutely without thought of the enormous responsibility that is his" (p. 111).

Sedgwick charged that sinister politicians were hiring the muckrakers. People were being found guilty before being investigated. Increased circulation had replaced responsibility. Magazines reflecting the new journalism were replacing daily newspapers as the molders of public opinion. In the battle for circulation their editors had lost all sense of responsibility (p. 112).

CHAPTER 10

Political Thought from World War I to 1973

I Introduction

FROM the era of World War I into the 1970s the United States has undergone profound economic changes that have in turn affected the intellectual, social, religious, and political life of the nation. Before World War I muckrakers and other social reformers were convinced that equal opportunity for all Americans could be developed within the constitutional framework of the American government. Their trust was based on a conviction that if the majority could see the logic concerning the fairness of this concept, they would demand that politics be rescued from the various machines and interests. Thus could be established a national town meeting in which would be served the well-being of every individual.[1]

II Greenwich Village

The Progressive movement was affected by puritanical concerns, as the campaign against liquor amply illustrates. Many progressives were inclined to be straitlaced insofar as other aspects of morality were concerned. With a moral radical code of ethics the young intellectuals of the World War I era made Greenwich Village in the heart of New York City their sanctuary. Repelled by the stodginess and hypocrisy of conservative middle-class society, they gained solace and nourishment at Mable Dodge's salon while they attempted to brush aside traditionalism and create a brave, new, more open world. They were largely of a generation of Ivy League students who had been trained in the pragmatism of William James and the instrumentalism of John Dewey. They also had been exposed to the communism of Marx, the concepts of Freud, and the nihilism of the anarchists. Like Veblen theirs was a revolt against the machine, the corporation, and the provincialism that remained in America. The uncertainty of a capitalistic society with neither social welfare programs nor social security made them both restless and insecure. Strikebreaking activities of corporations and various levels of government influenced their turn to the left. The solution of the young intellectuals oftimes was a variation of socialism and pacifism. Certainly not their leader but their brightest light was Randolph Bourne.[2]

III Randolph Bourne

Randolph Bourne was born in 1886 in Bloomfield, New Jersey, a small town a few miles from New York City. A deformity—a curvature of the spine—affected his life adversely. Middle-class affluent youth was replaced by financial hardship at the time that Bourne graduated from high school, and it was six years, filled with menial labor and job searching, before he entered Columbia University. His first serious reading of radical thought was Henry George's single-tax theory. His interest in such literature converted him to socialism. In college he became editor of the Columbia literary periodical and also began professional writing, contributing to the *Atlantic Monthly*. The radical opinions and feelings that he had for the less fortunate set him apart from the rest of the students. His work in graduate school under John Dewey was to have a major influence upon his thought. Dewey at the time was presenting a thesis concerning a new morality of business and materialism. These, according to the pragmatic philosopher, were not evil per se; what was needed was the proper attitude which fitted in with socialism. At this time Bourne published his first book, *Youth and Life*, in which he called upon youth to be the "advance guard in a drive for social progress and cultural enrichment."[3] Christopher Lasch has written that "not Marx but the spirit of Ponce de Leon presided over Bourne's vision of the better world."[4]

After a trip to Europe where he was impressed with the contrast between German orderliness and British slovenliness, Bourne began writing for the *New Republic*, espousing Dewey's pragmatism in his articles. For example, instead of being bound, as a typical Ivy Leaguer, to traditional classical education, Bourne was an early advocate of vocational training. He was particularly excited by Dr. Seaman Knapp's energy and genius in propagating in the open fields and among the farmers the principles of scientific farming, diversified crops, and home industry. Later, with the threat of involvement in World War I looming, Bourne was to suggest that instead of a military draft that there be a corps of youthful missionaries bringing expertise in the areas of health, gardening, and domestic science.[5]

Upon the entrance of the United States into the war a considerable number of American intellectuals enlisted as propagandists against the Germans. Bourne, courageously and steadfastly, remained a pacifist. When Dewey joined the prowar people, Bourne turned on his beloved professor with vengeance. He warned of the dangers of the government's stringent conformist policies.[6] His fight for peace provided continuity between Thoreau's pacifism during the Mexican War and that of the Vietnamese protesters.

IV *John Reed*

The glamor of Greenwich Village was greatly enhanced by John Reed, a native of Portland, Oregon. Reed came to the Village via Harvard. His transformation from a brassy overly aggressive college student to the golden boy of the Village has become a legend. Writing as a journalist in the impressionistic manner of Stephen Crane, he covered the International Workers of the World textile strike at Paterson, New Jersey, and was jailed during the episode. His next experience was in the Mexican Revolution as a war correspondent traveling with Pancho Villa. During World War I, after covering combat, his growing sympathy with radicalism brought him to Russia during the Revolution. He became involved there with both Lenin and Leon Trotsky. He recorded his view of the birth of the Soviet Union in *Ten Days That Shook the World* (1919). Possibly a hopeless romantic, he matured neither as a writer nor as a poet. But combining his activism, his sympathy with the downtrodden, his keen reporter's eye and pen, he is a major radical writer of the Village. Since he died relatively young in Russia, American Communists later created a myth from his saga.[7]

V *Walter Lippmann*

Assisting Croly as an editor of *The New Republic* was a fellow political writer whose career would span over half a century. Walter Lippmann, like his friend, John Reed, was a Harvard socialist who gravitated to Greenwich Village before World War I. Leaving socialism Lippmann became a strong supporter of the progressivism of Theodore Roosevelt in 1912 and later, during World War I, of Woodrow Wilson. His was a quest for stability in democracy with a commitment to a faith in the goodness of man. His first book, *A Preface to Politics* (1913), began his lifelong effort to reform American government. His odyssey would lead him from radicalism to liberalism to conservatism. In 1936 he would support Landon rather than Franklin Roosevelt as the lesser of two evils. A newspaper columnist for many years, and author of numerous books and articles, his views would have a profound influence on the American public including presidents.[8]

VI   *Historians and World War I Propaganda*

The spectacle of ivory-tower historians serving in the role of government propagandists during World War I sets the scene for a unique and tragic episode in American history. That an extremely capable and able university professor and administrator was president makes the event even more bizarre. The ivory tower ceased to exist during the war. A university was no longer the last sanctuary for those with critical minds. In a closed society conformity and hatred reigned supreme. Distinguished historians displayed all the integrity of Madison Avenue hacks as they turned out tracts for George Creel's Committee on Public Information. College administrators yielded to outside pressures and dismissed unpopular professors. What is most amazing is that Professor James T. Shotwell of Columbia University with a Quaker background would act as a catalyst for the episode.[9]

VII   *The 1920s*

Despite Wilson's idealism the crusade to make the world safe for democracy not only failed in Europe, but it undermined both freedom and democracy at home, particularly with the repression of both radicalism and liberalism. The revolt of the young intellectuals which had burned so brightly in Greenwich Village before the United States entered World War I was in a state of shambles. The Red Scare which followed the conflagration would also leave scars. Liberals, including Dewey, who had backed the war effort and Wilson, would accept the indictments by Bourne and other pacifists. Croly's *New Republic* would now go so far as to oppose the ratification of the Treaty of Versailles. The decade after World War I was one of both conservatism and Republican party domination, the same as the Reconstruction era. The Republicans, largely either remnants or followers of the Old Guard, generally supported, except for a protective tariff, a philosophy of laissez faire which amounted to the national administration's being an instrument of business. Farmers and workers were sacrificed for practically unrestricted favoritism toward big business. The Democrats, infiltrated by 1924 by the second Klan and dominated by their conservative southern wing, returned to the policy of "me too."

Some of the former progressives abandoned capitalism for socialism and Communism. Those who became Communists were inclined to see the Soviet Union as a veritable utopia. Others who remained progressives had their ranks buttressed by labor union leaders in a rebirth of the Bull Moose party. "Battle Bob" LaFollette ran as their candidate for president in 1924 with a platform that maintained that reformed capitalism not only would work but was needed.

VIII   *Henry L. Mencken*

As the days of William McKinley seemingly returned, among those who disparaged the "common man-Boobus Americanus" was the elitist Baltimore journalist and satirical essayist, Henry L. Mencken. His comment on Warren G. Harding during the presidential campaign of 1920 is typical of his cynicism:

Gamaliel [Harding] is the normal American of the better class—the more honest and reflective class. His thoughts are muddled, but profound. He speaks bad English, but he has a heart. He is the archtype of the Homo boobus. Put him into the White House and you will put every president of every Chamber of Commerce into the White House, and every chairman of every YMCA boobsqueezing drive, and every sales manager of every shoe-factory, and every reader of the *Saturday Evening Post* and every abhorrer of the Bolsheviki, and every Prominent Baltimorean.[10]

IX   *William Allen White and Will Rogers*

Perhaps the political writer who most realistically described the spirit of the 1920s was the veteran Emporia, Kansas, editor, William Allen White. With a career which reached back to strong opposition to the Populists in the 1890s, White later became a progressive with a few kind words for those agrarian rebels during Theodore Roosevelt's presidency: "Populism shaved its whiskers, washed its shirt, put on a derby and moved up into the middle of the class."[11] He regarded President Wilson as a man who attempted to play the role of God.

Still, in World War I White had joined the scholarly propagandists in decrying the ruthless ideals of the Germans.[12]

White clearly saw the mediocrity of the presidents who followed Wilson. First, there was Harding, a small-town politician who neither understood nor was understood by New York businessmen who preferred messenger boys to a prosperous small-town publisher whose thoughts lacked depth. Unable to separate himself from the comraderie of crooks and grafters, he was in the end destroyed by them (pp. 424–34).

Coolidge, according to White's description, was a Vermont Yankee, totally without experience in Washington when he arrived as vice-president. Since he completely lacked both initiative and leadership, his success rested largely on his *honesty* (pp. 435–47).

In *Colliers* for 9 August 1924 White evaluated the Presidential candidates of 1924: Calvin Coolidge, John Davis, and Robert LaFollette.[13] The Republican party he characterized "as a Union League Club in patriotic parade" (p. 7). In other words, it represented middle Anglo-Saxon America complete with the Chambers of Commerce, the Rotarians, and Calvin Coolidge. The Democrats were the eastern Irish, the southern cavaliers and the untamed spirits of the West. Their candidate John Davis was a Wilsonian liberal. The Democrats would attempt to capture the middle ground. On the left LaFollette was a lone fighter running without an organized party. The supporters of LaFollette included the farmers, the single tax people, organized labor, and "the dreamers among the foreign born" (pp. 8, 27). For the public there seemed "to be little difference between the liberal conservatism of Mr. Davis and the cautious conservatism of Mr. Coolidge" (pp. 7–8). It was obvious that White's sentiments were with LaFollette.

Few political writers have had the large and enthusiastic following of newspaper readers belonging to humorist Will Rogers. The former Oklahoma cowboy wrote both incisive and humorous comments on politics, starting with the Chicago Republican convention in 1920. His approach was an imaginary dialogue with veteran Old Guardsman Senator Boise Penrose of Pennsylvania. Penrose, like Rogers, was not present at the convention. The Democratic convention the same year, he likened to a Ouija board seance.[14]

In 1924 he attended the Democratic convention in New York and performed in the Ziegfield Follies, using political jokes as part of his repertoire. Many of his gags were typed on scraps of paper. His exasperation at poor leadership was at times not hidden by his poking fun at the proceedings (pp. 43–47).

X *The Southern Agrarians*

Just as Greenwich Village provided a sanctuary for intellectual radicals of the World War I era, Vanderbilt University became a haven for intellectual southern conservatives of the 1920s. Bourne, Reed, and the other Greenwich Village radicals had protested the dehumanization of the nation; the Nashville-based Agrarians tongue-lashed those who were dehumanizing the South. Their thesis was made with carefully intellectualized arguments. They revolted against the New South's headlong race for progress. They felt that the boosters were thrusting aside the traditional values in their headlong blind drive for profits. While the Agrarians idealized the yeoman farmer and the plantation aristocrat, unlike the Greenwich Villagers, they made little effort to identify with the underdogs of Dixie: the sharecroppers, the factory workers and the miners.

Perhaps the theme of their revolt was best expressed in Andrew Lytle's, "Throw out the radio and take down the fiddle from the wall."[15] Here was expressed a yearning for the past, a past that actually existed when they were young. And with that yearning was added a strong antipathy to the electronic dissonance of the airways. However, their largely fictional writing went far back into the past of the South, to the antebellum era and the Civil War. With pride they claimed that they were unreconstructed Southerners maintaining the barricades against the crass Philistines, particularly the nouveau riche industrialists and those who would follow the New South philosophy of Henry Grady.

Published in 1930, *I'll Take My Stand by Twelve Southerners* was both their manifesto and their bible as they attempted to persuade their southern readers to return to the myth of the Old South. In "Reconstructed But Unregenerate" John Crowe Ransome suggested that man should give up trying to conquer nature; instead, he should seek to achieve a truce.[16] Frank L. Owsley accused the North of having unfairly fixed the stigma of war guilt on the South. He also saw that the prime cause of the Civil War was not slavery but, rather, conflict "between the industrial and commercial civilization of the North and the agrarian civilization of the South."[17] This interpretation fitted well into the prime thesis of the Agrarians. Allen Tate cleverly separated protestantism from capitalism in persuading his viewers in "Remarks on the Southern Religion" that the faith of Calvin, Luther, and Wesley was that of a feudal society.[18] John Gould Fletcher in "Education Past and Present" went national in condemning education as being athletically rather than learning oriented.[19]

The Vanderbilt Agrarians were not activists. Most of them had no intention of abandoning their ivory tower for their cause. The Depression found them comfortably ensconced with their research and writing. Meanwhile, the New Deal would further change the South.

XI   *The Depression*

Congress in the 1920s evidenced a solicitude toward business that was not displayed toward other groups in the economy. Farmers and workers were sacrificed for practically unrestricted favoritism toward large business. However, from Grant to Hoover the gospel of economic individualism was preached by most presidents in moderate old-fashioned language which appealed greatly to the middle class.[20] Herbert Hoover's solicitude toward business was probably subconscious rather than rational. Still, when during the Great Depression Hoover championed individualism, self-help, and cooperation for the unemployed, these proved platitudes, not solutions to their plight.[21]

In the 1932 presidential election Hoover envisioned himself as Horatio defending the bridge over the Tiber. Speaking at Madison Square Garden, New York, 31 October, he admitted that the economic system had "received abnormal shocks during the last three years," but these shocks had been largely caused by world conditions. Hoover warned his listeners that the Democrats intended to do away with the traditional American social philosophy. Thus they would radically change the political, economic and social system of the nation.[22] This traditional system

is the product of our race and of our experience in building a nation to heights unparalleled in the whole history of the world. . . . It is founded on the conception that only through ordered liberty, through freedom to the individual, and equal opportunity to the individual will his initiative and enterprise be summoned to spur the march of progress.

It is by the maintenance of equality of opportunity and therefore of a society absolutely fluid in freedom of the movement of its human particle, that our individualism departs from the individualism of Europe. (p. 3)

Hoover was convinced that the keystone of the American system was voluntary cooperation within the community. Centralization of the government would destroy the American way of life. However, in times of emergency "the great reserve powers of the Federal Government shall be brought into action to protect the community. But when [the emergency ceases] . . . there must be a return of state, local, and individual responsibility" (p. 5).

With the continuation of the Great Depression from 1929 into 1932 businessmen were faced with a continuation of the laissez faire philosophy of let nature take its course. They had been hostile in the past toward Populism and progressivism but shaken by thoughts of disaster, they temporarily abandoned their conservatism. They had no rallying point, save a newly elected president[23] who affirmed that the "almost complete collapse of the American economic system . . . called for tearing down . . . many unsound structures, the adoption of new methods and a rebuilding from the bottom up."[24]

XII   *The New Deal*

Despite Hoover's dire predictions, the American public in 1932 was in a mood for a change. Hoover would have been defeated regardless of who ran against him. The urban appeal of Al Smith had been largely limited to the metropolitan areas of the East in 1928. His rejection by the powerful southern bloc ruled out his availability in 1932. So the Democratic party turned to a country squire, socially well-established, and currently governor of New York. Franklin Roosevelt came to the presidency prepared to come to grips with the Great Depression within the framework of the liberal faith.[25]

Spurred by the impact of technology and organization, the great economic interests had been advancing with supersonic speed while political concepts remained in a horse and buggy era, according to Charles A. Beard and George H.E. Smith, in *The Future Comes: A Study of the New Deal* (1933).[26] The New Deal was a time of catch up which would produce "tensions which must be adjusted by reason or force" (p. 169).

Rexford G. Tugwell in *The Battle for Democracy* (1935) gave depth to the thesis projected by Beard and Smith. A leading Brain Truster, and professor of economics at Columbia University, Tugwell saw the New Deal's objective as restoring "a workable exchangeability among the separate parts of our economic machine and" setting "it to functioning again; and beyond this to perfect arrangements which may prevent its future disorganization."[27] The New Deal was a democratic process, not laissez faire, revised to meet the necessities of a world economic system (p. 199).

Henry A. Wallace, secretary of agriculture in the first two New Deal administrations and later vice-president, reinforced Tugwell's theme in *Democracy Reborn* (1944). Answering the arguments of those who believed that one could not regiment nature, Wallace suggested that one "prepare for the whims of nature."[28]

For seventy years corporations had increasingly dominated the business and political sectors. During this time public opinion has been friendly toward corporations, and it would, Wallace felt, be a mistake to condemn all of them "as ruthless monsters seeking to plunder defenseless competitors and gouge the public."[29] However, the relationship of large corporations to the general welfare was a complicated problem (p. 125). He advocated replacing their individualistic attitudes with more enlightened ones which would eliminate "wide fluctuations in production, employment, savings and profits" (p. 124).

Veteran progressive Secretary of the Interior Harold Ickes, unlike Hoover, saw America's problems to be peculiarly her own.[30] Franklin Roosevelt was "a bold and resourceful leader," not afraid to innovate. The criticism that the New Deal broke away "from our old democratic moorings" was absurd (p. viii). Ickes felt that the Declaration of Independence should be properly understood in building a new social order committed to the greatest good for the greatest number (p. 74).

The new pragmatic philosophy of the New Deal strove to retain the political principles of constitutional government and the economic principles of an open competitive market yet extend the sphere of the federal government. Laissez faire capitalism would not be replaced by socialism. Attacks by Republicans were reminiscent of Whig and Know-Nothing accusations against Jacksonian Democracy, including the revival of the charge of un-Americanism.

President Roosevelt effectively defended his administration against attacks by Hoover and his allies on the right and by Senator Huey Long and Father Charles Coughlin of the radical fringe. He was not compelled to answer charges by Norman Thomas and the Socialists on the left.[31] Attacks by the far left Communists would only further popularize the New Deal.

Despite his overwhelming defeat in 1932, Hoover continued to assail the New Deal as an effort to shift the fundamental philosophic and social ideas of the United States. In *The Challenge to Liberty* (1934) he held that the emergency caused by the Great Depression did not justify this radical change. Responsibility for relief lay first with the individual; second, with institutional forces; third, with the local government; and finally, with the state government. Only when the capacities of all these had been exhausted, should the federal government intercede. However, no American willing to work should go hungry.[32]

Although Hoover approved of federal aid when all other measures had failed, to him certain New Deal projects were wasteful, futile, and corrupt. He also feared that the New Deal would be used for political purposes (pp. 106–7). Yet he realized that the Great Depression had brought to the surface weaknesses and abuses in the economic system: "Reform and revision of our older regulatory laws in banking, commodity and stock markets, transportation, utilities and natural resource industries are absolutely necessary" (p. 107).

He affirmed that American political leaders had been engaged both in planning and the execution of plans since the Washington administration. Projects had included public school systems, desert reclamation, the Panama Canal, and the Federal Reserve System. Further, the government had cooperated with the private sector in the building of railroads, airlines, and a merchant marine (p. 109). The rise of America was only partly due to its natural resources. It had also been stimulated by ideals and philosophic ideas with a maximum of free will in an ordered Liberty" (p. 111).

Instead of free will, the New Deal substituted "coercive National Planning" and "National Regimentation of our economic and social life" (p. 112). There were "transcendent obstacles" to the successful mixing of such ideas with democracy because they were "based upon wholly different conceptions of human rights which instantly clash" (p. 112).

Later, in *American Ideals versus the New Deal* (1936), Hoover warned Republicans that when the Whig party failed to come to grips with the issue of slavery, it disappeared. The issue was now freedom. Fundamental American liberties were at stake. Republicans should strongly make their commitment to freedom.[33]

As the presidential election of 1936 approached S. Wells Utley, president and general manager of the Detroit Steel Casting Company, in *The American System: Shall We Destroy It?* (1936) feared that the New Deal was ruining private enterprise. Also vice-president of the National Association of Manufacturers, Utley maintained that "under our system we get out of depressions by stimulating the hope and the opportunity for profit, by lowering prices rather than raising them, by decreasing taxes rather than increasing them, by stimulating men to labor and produce rather than by subsidizing them to remain in idleness."[34]

The role of the government in a depression was to practice strict economy, maintain peace, and defend property. Laws governing society were as fundamental and unchanging as laws governing phys-

ical science. If civilizations followed unsound principles they would
fall (p. 291). Further, ". . . remembering that there are innumerable
exceptions, the men who are unemployed today are the least efficient, the least industrious, the least intelligent, and the most shiftless element of our industrial population" (p. 268). Utley maintained
that a human right was given by God. Since jobs were man-made
institutions, they were not human rights (p. 269). The choice was
between a state collective security system or a personal competitive
enterprise system. These two were completely irreconcilable (p. 8).

James P. Warburg in *Hell Bent for Election* (1935) claimed that the
outcome in 1932 was an overwhelming vote against Hoover rather
than a vote for the Democratic candidate.[35] The record of fulfillment
of the New Deal kept the promises made by the Socialist candidate,
Norman Thomas (p. 5). On the other hand, Warburg charged that
Roosevelt's actions had been mostly ineffective. Further, he was
seeking to change the American way of life (p. 62). His main objective
was to remain president. Thus he could "adopt the Socialist platform
and deny its label" (p. 65).

Warburg found Roosevelt a deep thinker on party politics, but
"undeniably and shockingly superficial about anything that relates to
economics and particularly about anything that relates to finance" (p.
67). He charged that Roosevelt was "an ideal popular candidate for
office, but an ineffective and dangerous incumbent, once he is
elected" (p. 73).

XIII   *The Far Left*

The New Deal was attacked by both the far left and far right.
Longtime leader of American socialism, Norman Thomas, in *After
the New Deal, What?* in 1936 saw the program of the Roosevelt
administration in ashes. According to Thomas, three causes were
responsible for its demise. First, business no longer consented and
cooperated; second, the effect of adverse Supreme Court decisions;[36]
and third, the fact "that it did not perform its basic task in terms of
effective control of our economic and social order" (p. 13).

Earl Browder in *What is Communism* (1936) asserted that the
Communists claimed to be the rightful inheritors of "the revolutionary traditions of America." The New Deal he saw as strengthening
the federal government in order to increase profits for private business. He claimed that American finance capital supported the New
Deal. He also felt that New Deal policies "merely gave a new form to

the fundamental" policies of Hoover, Mellon and Coolidge which he called the "Old Deal."[37]

The Manifesto of the Communist Party., U.S.A. (1934) called the Wagner Act, the Civilian Conservation Corps, the Agricultural Adjustment Act and the National Recovery Act "fascist and war measures." It claimed that only the Communist party fought for the workers. The manifesto asserted that Wall Street was running the country. The great example which the toiling masses should follow was that of the Russian working class which had brought about a veritable utopia in the Soviet Union (pp. 240, 243).

XIV   *The Far Right*

On the far right both Senator Huey P. Long and Father Charles Coughlin would have scuttled the pragmatic patchwork of the New Deal for their own programs. In *My First Days in The White House* (1935), Long predicted a utopia with his election. No one would be "without comfort or employment."[38] In a series of radio lectures Father Charles Coughlin intimated that the New Deal was a "candy-coated pill." He asserted that there was "no panacea or nostrum which would restore America to prosperity."[39]

Coughlin's organization, the National Union for Social Justice, offered an alternative plan for recovery. First, an increased wage for the blue collared worker, then for the farmer a fair profit (p. 233). For the unemployed "a permanent public works program of reforestation, of land reclamation, of slum clearance, of national highway building . . ." (p. 236). For banking Coughlin projected a government owned central bank (p. 237), returning to the days of Nicholas Biddle, President Jackson, and the Bank of the United States.

Also on the far right Lawrence Dennis predicted in *The Coming of American Fascism* (1936) the demise of both capitalism and democracy. Both fascism and communism were crisis formulas. A trend toward fascism would prevent the United States from being involved in another "wild adventure" in Europe. Misguided American liberals would lead the United States into a crusade to replace Hitler with a Communist.[40]

XV   *The Atomic Bomb*

While the role of the United States domestically centered around a continuation of the New Deal, in the area of foreign affairs the United

States, during World War II, was thrust into the position of the foremost world power. This would involve atomic power, the formation of the United Nations, and later, the Marshall plan, along with the organization of regional alliances, such as the North Atlantic Treaty Organization.

No military decision made by the United States in its history has been as controversial as the use of the atomic bomb. Despite the shock felt by the American people caused by the sinking of the Lusitania by a German submarine in World War I, a shock caused primarily by the loss of life of noncombatants, particularly women and children, the decision was made by President Truman to drop atomic bombs on Hiroshima and Nagasaki, so as to more speedily bring about the surrender of Japan. The thinking behind the use of the bomb would be revealed in Henry L. Stimson's, "The Decision to Use the Atomic Bomb," in the February 1947 issue of *Harper's*. Stimson's chief justification was that the bomb ended the war, thus preventing "the ghastly specter of a clash of great land armies," the further fire bombing of cities, and the continuation of the blockade of Japan.[41]

Later, in *Japan Subdued* (1961), veteran foreign affairs expert Herbert Feis would reinforce Stimson's view in the great debate which ensued. Feis claimed that since the bomb was not banned by explicit international agreement, the dropping was justified. He did feel, however, that the United Sates should have advised the Japanese government of its tremendous destructive power before its use.[42]

Opposition to the use of the bomb came from a variety of sources. Hanson W. Baldwin, the military editor of the *New York Times*, strongly criticized its dropping. In a volume entitled *Great Mistakes of the War* (1949) Baldwin held that Japan was prostrate at the time the bomb was used. Further, when the United States utilized the bomb it accepted the premise of total war. In doing so we lost to the doctrine of exigency, the preeminent moral position which we once held. *Commonweal*, a moderate intellectual independent Catholic periodical, condemned without reservation the dropping of the bomb.[43] This would be the view of many Americans, shocked by the exigencies of war.

XVI *Conservatism versus Liberalism*

During World War II the United States emerged from the Great Depression. Most social and economic reforms of the New Deal were continued. The major domestic issue came to be whether the federal government should use its power and resources to accomplish further social and economic objectives. The position that one took on this issue was one measurement of whether one was a liberal or conservative. The general disposition of the liberals is to approve of such use, of the conservatives to disapprove.[44]

Senator Robert Taft would now be the major spokesman of the conservatives.[45] On his death they would shift to Senator Barry Goldwater. Conservatives feared that the idea of a welfare state together with the decline in morality would lead to totalitarianism. Leading postwar conservative political writers included Russell Kirk and Peter Viereck.

Kirk, the most important figure in postwar conservatism, selected six canons of conservative thought in *The Conservative Mind* (1953). His philosophy emphasized order, property, and freedom. Change should be slow and conserving. Rejecting universal suffrage, his was an elitist approach with man's returning to religion.[46]

According to Kirk in *A Program for Conservatives* (1954), liberalism was now looked on with suspicion. The two world wars had hurt it, and the pragmatism of John Dewey was dead. The alternative, conservatism, was not an ideology. The conservative simply looked at political, economic, religious, and ethical problems as part and parcel of the whole.[47]

Peter Viereck in *Conservatism Revisited* (1962) attempted to define and survey "conservatism in its cultural context of classicism and humanism."[48] Viereck saw most liberals as being unsympathetic toward Communism. On the other hand, most conservatives were not advocates of a dictatorship (p. 23). The core of conservatism was "a humanist reverence for the dignity of the individual soul" (p. 33).

Ronald Lora perceives Viereck as having achieved a synthesis of philosophical conservatism and political liberalism. To Lora Viereck is, at most, a fellow traveler of liberalism who embodies "the rationally humane sentiments of the New Conservatism."[49]

American Communism had been affiliated with the Soviet Union from its beginnings. Free institutions in a free society seemingly made the United States vulnerable to the tactic of infiltration.[50] To investigate not only Communism but also far right movements, the House Committee to investigate Un-American Activities came into existence in 1938.[51]

Following the Know-Nothing tradition, a number of conservatives rallied to the support of Senator Joseph McCarthy and the House Un-American Activities Committee. Such conservatives received strong support from William F. Buckley, Jr., founder and editor of the *National Review*. From a wealthy family and private school educated, Buckley graduated from Yale in 1950 and joined the ranks of conservatives a year later with his *God and Man at Yale*. As editor of the *National Review* he blended laissez faire conservatism with a crusade against Communism which the *National Review* labeled "Satanic Utopianism."[52]

In his defense of the House Un-American Activities Committee, William F. Buckley, Jr., claimed that following World War II, to allege that one was a Communist or an organization Communistic, opened one to the charge of being a "witch-hunter."[53] Though there was general indifference to the problem, the Soviet world threat was real and any "distinction between the internal and external threat" unreal.

Although Buckley strongly defended the term "un-American," he did concede that what would be un-American today might not have been un-American yesterday or un-American tomorrow. However, today, un-American should be used in relation to extremists of both left and right. On the other hand, in the historical sense white racism was despicable but not un-American (pp. 14–15, 24). Despicable ideas should "be disciplined by the market place" (p. 24). Un-American movements should be monitored and the committee's name changed to the House Committee on Communist Activities (p. 25).

Despite the support of Buckley and other conservatives, many defenders of freedom felt that the Un-American Activities Committee and Senator McCarthy were using undemocratic methods. These methods included guilt by association, failure to protect the citizen against the government, and stamping out freedom through the specious claim of promoting security.[54]

The traditional liberal tradition was maintained by Henry Steele Commager, Louis Hartz, and Arthur M. Schlesinger, Jr. In *The American Mind* (1950) Commager maintained "that there is a distinctively American way of thought, character, and conduct."[55] He saw the twentieth-century American as "more democratic than his nineteenth-century forbears . . ." (p. 408). However, the establishment of the House Un-American Activities Committee gave intolerance "the stamp of official approval" (p. 413).

Those who seemingly supported the Constitution and Declaration of Independence were, according to Commager, unfamiliar with both documents. Conformity and loyalty to them were synonymous. All, including genius, were required to conform to a pattern (pp. 413–14).

In addition business identified its "version of private enterprise with Americanism" (p. 413).

Hartz in *The Liberal Tradition in America* (1955) interpreted "the embroidering of the Bolshevik menace" as a natural technique for those in the old Whig tradition who attempted to discredit their opponents by labeling them socialists and un-American.[56] Hartz saw the United States as predominantly liberal from its inception.[57]

Schlesinger in *The Age of Jackson* (1946) stressed that democracy placed a premium "on tolerance, bargaining and compromise."[58] "The great tradition of American liberalism," he concluded, "regards man as neither brute nor angel" (p. 523). Following this line of thought in 1949, Schlesinger formulated a tough-minded liberalism. This involved a commitment to "contain the ideologies of the Right and the Left. . . ."[59]

In *The Affluent Society* (1958) John Kenneth Galbraith perceived the liberals abandoning as their major issue their classical program: "redistribution of the existing income, greater economic security," and protection of liberty from concentrated economic power. Influenced by the British economist John Maynard Keynes, after 1936 liberals took as their main theme high production and high employment. This new economic creed, according to Galbraith, would emphasize quantity, not quality.[60]

XVII *The Civil Rights Revolt*

After three decades in which the institution of segregation became the way of life in the South, conservatives recognized in the 1930s that there were aspects of egalitarianism in the New Deal that ran counter to "Jim Crow." Then, during World War II, the Swedish sociologist Gunnar Myrdal, with the aid of a staff of American researchers and writers, compiled the epic *An American Dilemma* (1944). In this monumental study, Myrdal documented proof of both the failure and the unfairness of the "separate but equal" doctrine contained in the *Plessy* v. *Ferguson* decision of 1896.[61]

During the 1940s, neo-Populist southern politician Jim Folsom of Alabama and New Dealer Claude Pepper of Florida recognized that votes for candidates regardless of color counted equally. In 1948 President Truman placed the national Democratic party squarely behind civil rights. The Dixiecrat revolt which carried four deep South states consisted of a combination of conservatives and white racists. Then in 1954 in a landmark decision the Supreme Court struck down school segregation as a de jure institution: "We conclude that in the field of public education the doctrine of 'separate but equal' has no place. Separate educational facilities are inherently unequal. Therefore, . . . the plaintiffs . . . are, by reason of the segregation complained of, deprived of the equal protection of the laws guaranteed by the Fourteenth Amendment."[62]

The National Association for the Advancement of Colored People (NAACP) supported the plaintiffs in the Brown decision. Since its formation in 1909 it had led in the furthering of civil rights.

In the year following the Brown decision, a strong indictment of the institution of segregation was made by C. Vann Woodward, one of the most respected historians of the post–World War II era. Woodward's thesis in *The Strange Career of Jim Crow* (1955) was that segregation in the South had its legal roots in laws passed two decades after the end of Reconstruction. He saw the prime reason for the South's adoption of extreme racism was the collapse of the various Federal and state restraining forces of the post-Reconstruction era. Following the Brown decision, Woodward credited further gains by the blacks to young black idealists led by Martin Luther King.[63]

A number of the foremost American writers would support both the conclusions of Myrdal and Woodward along with the Brown decision. Robert Penn Warren, a former Vanderbilt agrarian, in *Segregation: The Inner Conflict in the South* (1956) emphasized the inner guilt feelings of southerners.[64] Willie Morris, former editor-in-chief of *Harper's Magazine*, described in a deeply personal fashion the integration of the schools of his home town in the Mississippi delta. *Yazoo* (1971) carefully combined Morris's belief in a higher law with his understanding of southern conservatism.[65]

New Left historian and political scientist Howard Zinn, writing from the perspective of a northern white civil rights advocate on the faculty of a black institution in the South, described in *The Southern Mystique* (1964) the tenacious hold that segregation had on the South. Utilizing primarily a narrative frame of reference, Zinn endeavored to explain the hearts and minds of southerners, both white and black. The South he saw as a microcosm similar in basic aspects to the entire United States.[66]

XVIII   *Black Civil Rights Writers*

At the outset of the Montgomery bus boycott in 1955, it was strongly suspected by white Alabamians that the NAACP was behind the incident. It was also felt that the NAACP had close ties with the Communist party. Thus, it was a shock when it was discovered that the leader of the blacks was Martin Luther King, pastor of a middle-class church. King had not been active in the NAACP. Largely by means of his speeches, later published in *Stride Toward Freedom* (1958) and *Why We Can't Wait* (1964), King advocated civil rights using Thoreau's nonviolent theme. His letter to eight white Alabama clergymen from the Birmingham jail in 1963 was a most powerful and persuasive epistle emphasizing both nonviolence and Christian charity.[67]

A different, more radical approach, to the realization of equal rights was taken by Stokely Carmichael, a strong proponent of black power, who in 1966 became leader of the Student Non-Violent Coordinating Committee. The following year, in collaboration with Charles V. Hamilton, an academician, Carmichael wrote *Black Power: The Politics of Liberation in America* (1967). In it Carmichael and Hamilton rejected traditional democratic procedures and advocated a revolutionary posture.[68]

Earlier, James Baldwin in *Nobody Knows My Name* (1961) strongly protested against the stereotyped image of the inferior southern black complete with a savage African background. Writing with intense feeling, Baldwin evidenced unusually keen insight into the problems of race relations. His interview with William Faulkner brilliantly discerned the fallacies of the approach of conservative southerners, who cried "go slow" while attempting to hold onto their outmoded social structure. Baldwin bitterly asserted that little progress for the blacks in the South had come through the efforts of white southerners.[69]

The Autobiography of Malcolm X (1964) approached the civil rights revolt from the viewpoint of a black ghetto leader who had rejected Christianity in his search for identity. Malcolm X was in revolt against white racism. His objective was the recognition of the black as an integral part of the American culture.[70]

XIX *Segregationist Writers*

While most political writers favored integration, segregation had its strong supporters. These included John W. Davis, who represented the southern states in the Brown decision. Davis, a leading constitutional lawyer, had been the Democratic candidate for president in 1924. Another supporter was Carleton Putnam, a northern business executive turned writer. In *Race and Reason* (1961) he rested his argument for segregation on freedom of association. He also revived the old proslavery argument concerning the lack of a black civilization in Africa. For Locke's concept of natural law and inherent rights Putnam substituted the doctrine of earned rights with white society possessing veto power. He defended discrimination against exceptional blacks on the grounds that "discrimination of this sort was necessary to the practical administration of human affairs."[71]

Peter Carmichael, a long-time southern professor of philosophy and a former moderate, endeavored in *The South and Segregation* (1965) to support "Jim Crow" by utilizing legal, logical, and scientific arguments. Like Putnam he relied heavily on freedom of association, asserting that there was a logical racial aversion of whites to blacks that was not prejudice. Thus a state had the right to segregate.[72]

Joe Azbell, a southern journalist, in *The Riotmakers* (1968) saw the civil rights revolt as a black revolution engineered by Communists. Azbell pointed out that while the white world was integrated, private black facilities such as cafes, motels, and theaters remained black.[73] Insofar as Communism was concerned Putnam also felt that the Communists had "made the integration movement a part of their conspiracy. . . ."[74]

Politically, the segregationists would have their last hurrah with Goldwater in 1964 and Wallace in 1968. The Nixon and Ford Administrations would put the issue on a back burner. Carter would treat the issue of integration as a major issue but with a moderation that would be unacceptable to black militants.

XX   *The New Left*

Born during the civil rights revolt, the New Left replaced Marxism and liberalism with pragmatic radicalism. Its political power climaxed with massive demonstrations opposing the Vietnamese War. To the intellectual community the New Left philosophy appeared to be a blend of pacifism, humanitarianism, existentialism, and Marxism. Often substituting action for rhetoric, New Left academicians carried on an iconoclastic revolt against universities which proscribed dissent and encouraged conformity. They castigated those intellectuals who, frightened by the McCarthy witch-hunts and the rise of Goldwater conservatism, found safe ground on the right. Their movement, as they perceived it, was a moral crusade against paternalistic power elite.[75] Leading New Left political writers included William Apple-man Williams, Howard Zinn, Herbert Marcuse, and Tom Hayden.

XXI *Vietnamese Conflict*

Unlike Korea, which was a forgotten bailiwick of the United States after World War II, independence for South Vietnam became an American crusade after the fall of Dien Bien Phu in 1954. The letterhead of the American Friends of Vietnam, founded the follow-ing year, listed a number of prominent names, including Socialist Norman Thomas and liberal intellectuals Max Lerner and Arthur Schlesinger, Jr.[76] Later, the organization was headed by Henry Cabot Lodge and General Maxwell Taylor.[77] Cardinal Spellman placed the Catholic Church solidly behind the Diem regime in Vietnam. Dr. Tom Dooley with covert Eisenhower administration support in *Deliver Us From Evil* (1956) provided strong justification for the intervention of the United States to prevent South Vietnam from going Communist.

After a decade of military, economic, and advisory assistance came the highly controversial Gulf of Tonkin Senate resolution amounting to a declaration of war. In *The Vantage Point* (1971) President Lyndon Johnson gives a simplistic version of what occurred, making the decision a reaction to overt aggression by the North Vietnamese Communists.[78]

In no other war in which the United States has been involved, has there been as strong a base of opposition, including not only brilliant writers but also many of the young of America. The mystery of the Far East and of Vietnam in particular would be clarified in *Fire in the Lake* (1972) by Frances Fitzgerald, a journalist and scholar. Fitzgerald, a dove, has a basic understanding of the peasant society of Vietnam, Confucianism, and the highly unstable situation there brought on by modernization.[79]

Bernard Fall, a professor of international relations at Howard University and a Frenchman who was a long time expert on Vietnam, wrote in December 1965 in *Ramparts*, "This isn't Munich, it's Spain." Fall envisioned the war as being armed peasants versus Detroit and the "think factories." He also castigated the statement of former Secretary of State Dean Acheson that the objectives of a free society justified any means that contributed to those ends.[80]

In two volumes, the first narrative, the second more massive and analytical, David Halberstam followed the same frame of reference of

Fall and Fitzgerald. *The Making of a Quagmire* (1964) is the account of a war correspondent who sought the truth, bucked White House and Pentagon pressures, and viewed the early Vietnamese leader, Ngo Dinh Diem, as a materialistic anti-Communist mandarin who was unable to cope with the situation. In *The Best and the Brightest* (1969) Halberstam strongly indicted the hardliners in the Washington bureaucracy who thought that the war could be won by quantitative action without taking into consideration the culture of Vietnam.

Few American intellectuals have had the background concerning Vietnam of hawk Wesley Fishel, who served as an advisor to both the Vietnamese government and the United States. In *Vietnam: Anatomy of a Conflict* (1968), he warned the United States to take a careful look at its policy of counterinsurgency. A personal friend of Diem and leader of a Michigan State University team of scholars and public administration experts in Vietnam, Fishel early saw the weaknesses of the new military-civilian regime that succeeded the assassinated Diem.[81]

The divisiveness of the involvement in Vietnam was ably expressed by McGeorge Bundy, a former aide to Presidents Kennedy and Johnson, in "Gray is the Color of the Complex Truth" (1967). By 1967 reaction to the war had reached massive proportions in the United States. Bundy warned that the truth in Vietnam was not easy to reach. A settlement would also depend on Hanoi. The dissention at home would have its effect up there. He called for "human sympathy across political difference" and for moderation.

Fresh to the presidency in 1969, Nixon planned to buy time in Vietnam by continued heavy bombing and by maintaining ground troops, though at reduced levels. There was now a general feeling that the South Vietnamese defense forces could never be made capable of withstanding an invasion from the north. It was at this time that a former hawk and veteran government consultant on Vietnam, Daniel Ellsberg, decided to release top secret Department of Defense documents.[82] Appearing in the *New York Times*, they became known as the Pentagon Papers.[83] Ellsberg—who had previously worked on other confidential projects—defended his decision in *Papers on the War* (1972). He justified his breach of security on the grounds that the war was both a foreign aggression and criminal. His act, according to him, helped free his fellow Americans from the conflict.[84]

XXII *Politics After 1959*

Not since the reelection of Theodore Roosevelt in 1904 had the United States experienced the candidacy of a charismatic intellectual young Ivy League politician. Theodore White, in *The Making of the President, 1960*, measured Kennedy tempo with a penetrating analysis of the campaign. White struggled with Nixon, leaving an interpretation of his character to later writers.[85] The Camelot image would be projected early by Kennedy aides Theodore Sorenson and Arthur Schlesinger, Jr. Sorenson, in *Kennedy* (1965), credited him with both style and substance as an extraordinary man. His handling of Kennedy the man is discreet.[86]

Harvard professor Arthur Schlesinger, Jr., would become the intellectual in residence of the Kennedy Administration. His *A Thousand Days* (1965) combined excellent writing, careful documentation, and a strong admiration of Kennedy. His last chapter, Autumn 1963, sets the scene for Camelot. His interpretation of Kennedy was that he "opened up a new era in the American political consciousness."[87]

If Kennedy's Camelot had a dragon, it was Senator Barry Goldwater of Arizona. In *The Conscience of a Conservative* (1960) Goldwater presented the Republicans with a conservative philosophy which was pre-McKinley, except in advocacy of a strong national defense and the nonrecognition of the Soviet Union. Nonrecognition of a country whose government was repugnant to the United States was of Wilsonian origin. Goldwater advocated the repeal of the New Deal and once again making welfare the province of private charity. His simplistic philosophy pitted individual self-reliance against state paternalism.[88]

Tom Wicker, Washington bureau chief of the *New York Times*, in *JFK and LBJ: The Influence of Personality upon Politics* (1968) evaluated the two presidents who dominated the 1960s. He saw Kennedy as attempting the role of a strong liberal president but frustrated by the Congress and the Bay of Pigs. Wicker identified Johnson as a southerner, bringing not only the South but the blacks to equal status in the Union. At a time of domestic violence and the Vietnam War he attempted to achieve a consensus.[89]

The Politics of Consensus (1968) would be the title of a book by Sidney Hyman which would not only explain the role of consensus in

American politics, but would advocate it as the political philosophy most desired for the future. Thus Hyman insisted that a consensus such as President Johnson sought to achieve was imperative for the United States.[90] Princeton professor Eric Goldman, in *The Tragedy of Lyndon Johnson* (1969), examined the triumphs and failures of the Johnson administration. Goldman, who was the "intellectual in residence" at the White House, found Johnson to be a profoundly complex man. Despite his background of Senate leader and vice-president, Goldman felt that Johnson was too seriously flawed in personal characteristics to be an engaging public figure. Though he was successful with programs, he could not command the respect necessary for leadership.[91]

The presidential election in 1968 would be brilliantly and deftly described in *An American Melodrama* (1969) by three English reporters, Lewis Chester, Godfrey Hodgson, and Bruce Page. As closely as possible they achieved objectivity. They saw the most disturbing problem in American politics to be the gap between rhetoric and reality.[92]

Following the election—in which the Republicans carried a majority of southern states—Kevin Phillips, an assistant to John Mitchell, wrote *The Emerging Republican Majority* (1969), in which he predicted a political future that would be increasingly conservative and increasingly Republican, a forecast certainly substantiated by the 1972 election.[93] A different projection was made by the Ripon Society in *The Lessons of Victory* (1969). The Cambridge, Massachusetts, based organization endeavored to support a program that would bridge the gap between the Republicans and the intellectuals.[94]

Perhaps the most complex politician in our history has been Richard Nixon. In *Nixon Agonistes* (1970), journalist Garry Wills penned a penetrating evaluation of his strengths and weaknesses at the outset of his presidency. Wills described with painstaking detail and detachment the rise of a young hardworking lawyer, "a brooding Irish puritan," a post–World War II man who practiced the politics of resentment.[95] *Nixon Agonistes* is required background reading for anyone attempting to understand Nixon's role in the Watergate episode.

CHAPTER 11

Conclusion

FROM 1800 to the present, influenced by economic, social, religious, and intellectual factors, as well as governmental, American political writers have dealt with their topics in a variety of ways. Despite considerable change since 1800 the two basic documents of American political law have remained the Constitution and the Declaration of Independence. Only a handful of writers on the far right and far left would eliminate these. The Constitution has as its theme life, liberty, and property; the Declaration of Independence calls for life, liberty, and the pursuit of happiness. Both are fundamental to an overview of our political evolution as seen through the various writers. By defining conservatism versus liberalism and basically a conflict between property rights and human rights, one can best understand the split legacy of the right and the left.

Effects of the Industrial Revolution and the New Deal have made Jefferson's less government philosophy more acceptable to the conservatives, while Hamilton's leviathan state is more pleasing to liberals. The shifting role of the federal government from proponent of laissez faire capitalism to the concept of the welfare state has led to the substitution of collectivism for individualism, the common good for liberty.

In supporting their respective positions, American political writers have always borrowed generously from both European forerunners and counterparts. In 1800 these included Hobbes, Locke, Voltaire, Rousseau, and Montesquieu. After the Civil War, Darwin, the Manchester liberals, and Marx would add to the depth of American political writing. De Tocqueville and Lord Bryce, both visitors to our shores, would have a strong impact.

American political writers, particularly reformers and extremists, have at times tended to exaggerate differences, thus concealing any consensus which exists at the time. The opposition, whether in or out of power, is by these people accused of being an elite, such as the slave power or Wall Street, and callous insofar as the common good is

151

concerned. There has been in the past an acceptance of the thesis identifying the common good with the righteousness of the United States and the rule of a higher, moral law. This thesis underwent a shattering experience with the dropping of the atomic bomb on Japan.

Darwin's belief in the survival of the fittest provided a philosophy supportive of the rise of the large corporations. It also reinforced the frontier love of freedom and the white southerner's belief in the inferiority of the black. It was to become a strong component of conservative thinking. On the other hand, the revolt of the Populists was the first major challenge to this thesis, a challenge that would later be taken up by the progressives and then the New Deal. Conflict in political writing between the conservatives, who emphasized liberty, individualism, states' rights, and materialism, and the liberals, who claimed to support the common good and the rights of the disadvantaged, continues to the present. The New Left has as its prime objective the replacement of American liberalism with its radicalism.

Issues of today largely reflect the role of the United States in world affairs and the domestic economy. The solutions of the moderate conservatives and liberals are remarkably similar. As late as 1955 Clinton Rossiter defined the American right as liberal in idealism and rhetoric but "conservative in mood and practice."[1] Thus it is certain that the conflict between liberals and conservatives will continue. The desire for upward mobility in a land rich in natural resources has provided much incentive for both liberals and conservatives alike in their continuous political struggle. Thus the conflict between those who support the concept of the greatest good for the greatest number against those who believe that individual liberty and private property are more important continues today.

Notes and References

Chapter One

1. Ralph Gabriel, *The Course of American Democratic Thought* (New York: Ronald Press, 1956), p. 12.
2. Wilfred E. Binkley, *American Political Parties*, 4th ed. (New York: Alfred A. Knopf, 1962), p. 29.
3. Ronald Lora, *Conservative Minds in America* (Chicago: Rand McNally, 1971), p. 27.
4. Peter Viereck, *Conservatism from John Adams to Churchill* (Princeton: D. Van Nostrand, 1956), p. 94.
5. Paul Leicester Ford, ed., *The Writings of Thomas Jefferson*, 10 vols. (New York: G. P. Putnam's, 1892–1899), 2:3.
6. Henry H. Simms, *Life of John Taylor* (Richmond: William Byrd Press, 1932), p. 98.
7. John Taylor, *Arator: Being a Series of Agricultural Essays, Practical and Political* (Petersburg: 1818), p. vi.
8. Ibid., pp. 48, 50, 52, 54–55, 218–19.
9. Manning Dauer and Hans Hammond, "John Taylor: Democrat or Aristocrat," *The Journal of Politics* 6 (November 1944), 386, 403; Vernon Louis Parrington, *Main Currents in American Thought*, 2 vols. (New York: Harcourt Brace, 1927), 2:16.
10. Parrington, *Main Currents*, 2:14–15.
11. John Taylor, *An Inquiry into the Principles and Policy of the Government of the United States* (Fredericksburg: Green and Cady, 1814), pp. 550–51.
12. Merle Curti, *The Growth of American Thought*, 2d ed. (New York: Harper & Row, 1951), pp. 186–87.
13. *Dictionary of American Biography*, eds. Allen Johnson and Dumas Malone (New York: Charles Scribner's, 1936), s.v. "Ames, Fisher," by Samuel Eliot Morison.
14. Fisher Ames, "Intellect in a Democracy," in *The Prose Writers of America*, ed. Rufus W. Griswold (Philadelphia: A. Hart, 1852), p. 99.
15. Parrington, *Main Currents*, 1:275.
16. Ames, "An Essay," p. 96.
17. Fisher Ames, *Works of Fisher Ames* (Boston: T. B. Wait, 1809), pp. 388–89.
18. *Dictionary of American Biography*, s.v. "Ames."
19. *The Port Folio*, 3 (April 23, 1803), 135.
20. Joseph Dennie, *The Lay Preacher*, ed. Milton Ellis (New York, 1943), p. 147.

21. Curti, *American Thought*, p. 192.

22. William Cobbett, *Porcupine's Works; Containing Various Writings and Selections, Exhibiting a Faithful Picture of the United States of America* (London: Cobbett and Morgan, 1801), pp. 216–17.

23. Parrington, *Main Currents*, 2:19.

24. Ibid., 2:19–25.

25. *The Trustees of Dartmouth College* v. *Woodward* (1819) 4 Wheaton (U.S.) 518.

26. *McCulloch* v. *Maryland* (1819) 4 Wheaton (U.S.) 316.

27. Perry Miller, *The Life of the Mind in America from the Revolution to the Civil War* (New York: Harcourt, Brace & World, 1965), p. 219.

28. Mathew Carey, *The Olive Branch* (Philadelphia: M. Carey, 1815), p. 15.

29. Mathew Carey, *The New Olive Branch* (Philadelphia: M. Carey, 1820), pp. 108–9.

30. Mathew Carey, *Addresses of the Philadelphia Society for the Promotion of National Industry*, 6th ed. (Philadelphia: n.p., 1822), p. 10.

Chapter Two

1. *Boston Quarterly Review*, January 1839, pp. 123–25.

2. *The Political Mirror or Review of Jacksonism* (New York: J. P. Peaslee, 1835), p. 310.

3. Arthur M. Schlesinger, Jr., *The Age of Jackson* (Boston: Little, Brown, 1946), pp. 307–08.

4. Robert Mayo, *Political Sketches of Eight Years in Washington* (Baltimore: Fielding Lucas, 1839), pp. v–vi.

5. Grimes, *American Political Thought*, rev. ed. (New York: Holt, Rinehart and Winston, 1960), p. 185.

6. Schlesinger, *The Age of Jackson*, pp. 186–87.

7. William Leggett, *A Collection of the Political Writings of William Leggett*, ed. Theodore Sedgwick, Jr., 2 vols. (New York: Taylor & Dodd, 1840), 1:68.

8. Thomas P. Abernethy, *From Frontier to Plantation in Tennessee: A Study in Frontier Democracy* (University, Ala.: University of Alabama Press, 1967), pp. 242–43.

9. . William Leggett, *Collection*, 1:43.

10. David Crockett, *The Life of Martin Van Buren*. 10th ed. (Philadelphia: Robert Wright, 1836), pp. 166–67.

11. David Crockett, *An Account of Col. Crockett's Tour to the North and Down East, in the year of our Lord one thousand eight hundred and thirty four* (Philadelphia: Carey and Hart, 1835), pp. 48–49.

12. David Crockett, *Col. Crockett's Exploits and Adventures in Texas* (Philadelphia: Collins, 1836), pp. 56–59.

13. *Speech of Colonel Benj. Fanevil Hunt of Charleston, South Carolina, Delivered at the Request of the Democratic Republican General Committee at the Mass Meeting of the Mechanics and Working Men of New York, in reply to the Doctrines of Daniel Webster on the Currency and a National Bank* (New York: James Rees, 1840).

14. Ibid.

15. Hugh A. Garland, *An Oration, Pronounced in Castle Garden, July 27, 1840, in Celebration of the Second Declaration of Independence, or The Passage of the Independent Treasury Bill* (New York: William G. Boggs, 1840).

16. T. R. Hazard, *Facts for the Laboring Man by a Laboring Man* (Newport, R.I.: James Atkinson, 1840).

Chapter Three

1. Thomas Jefferson to John Holmes, 22 April 1820, in *The Portable Thomas Jefferson* (New York: Viking Press, 1975), pp. 567–68.

2. Louis Filler, *The Crusade Against Slavery 1830–1860* (New York: Harper, 1960), pp. 18–19.

3. John C. Calhoun, "Speech on the Reception of Abolition Petitions, February, 1837," in *Speeches of John C. Calhoun, Delivered in the Congress of the United States from 1811 to the Present Time* (New York: Harper, 1843), pp. 222–25.

4. *Dictionary of American Biography*, s.v. "Dew, Thomas Roderick," by Broadus Mitchell.

5. Thomas Roderick Dew, *An Essay on Slavery*, 2d ed. (Richmond: J. W. Randolph, 1849), p. 3.

6. *Dictionary of American Biography*, s.v. "Harper, William," by J. G. deR. Hamilton.

7. *The Pro-Slavery Argument, as Maintained by the Most Distinguished Writers of the Southern States, Containing the Several Essays, on the subject of Chancellor Harper, Governor Hammond, Dr. Simms and Professor Dew* (Charleston: Walker, Richards, 1852), pp. 14, 19.

8. *Dictionary of American Biography*, s.v. "Hammond, James Henry," by J. G. deR. Hamilton.

9. *The Pro-Slavery Argument*, p. 100.

10. Simms, "The Morals of Slavery," in *The Pro-Slavery Argument*, p. 178.

11. *Biographical Directory of the American Congress 1774–1971* (1971), s.v. "Grayson, William John."

12. William J. Grayson, *The Hireling and the Slave, Chicora, and Other Poems* (Charleston: McCarter, 1856), pp. 22, 50.

13. *Dictionary of American Biography*, s.v. "Fitzhugh, George," by Broadus Mitchell.

14. George Fitzhugh, *Cannibals All! or Slaves Without Masters* (Richmond: A. Morris, 1857), pp. 29–30.

15. This point of view is expressed in Francis Butler Simkins, *A History of the South*, 3d ed. (New York: Alfred A. Knopf, 1963), p. 191. See also Louis Schade, *A Book for the "Impending Crisis!"* in chap. 4.

16. Kenneth M. Stampp, *The Peculiar Institution: Slavery in the Ante-Bellum South* (New York: Vintage Books, 1956), pp. 422–24. This is an excellent study of American slavery.

Chapter Four

1. *The Liberator*, 1 January 1831.

2. Ibid.

3. James G. Birney, *A Letter on the Political Obligations of Abolitionists with a Reply by William Lloyd Garrison* (Boston: Dow & Jackson, 1839), p. 3.

4. *Dictionary of American Biography*, s.v. "Goodell, William," by W. Randall Waterman.

5. William Goodell, *Slavery and Anti-Slavery. A History of the Great Struggle in Both Hemispheres, with a View of the Slavery Question in the United States* (New York: William Harned, 1852), p. 560.

6. *Dictionary of American Biography*, s.v. "Channing, William Ellery," by Samuel M. Crothers.

7. William E. Channing, *The Works of William E. Channing, D. D.*, vol. 2 (Boston: James Munroe, 1841), p. 7.

8. Filler, *Crusade Against Slavery*, p. 33.

9. Channing, *Works*, 2:132.

10. Filler, *Crusade Against Slavery*, p. 128.

11. Ibid., p. 206.

12. Frederick Douglass, *Oration, Delivered in Corinthian Hall, Rochester, July 4th, 1852* (Rochester: Lee, Mann, 1852).

13. Arthur Young Lloyd, *The Slavery Controversy: 1831–1860* (Chapel Hill, University of North Carolina Press, 1939), p. 279.

14. Filler, *Crusade Against Slavery*, p. 207.

15. Lysander Spooner, *The Unconstitutionality of Slavery* (Boston: Bela Marsh, 1845), pp. 5–8.

16. Filler, *Crusade Against Slavery*, pp. 221–22.

17. Cassius M. Clay, *The Writings of Cassius Marcellus Clay including Speeches and Addresses*, ed., with preface and memoir, by Horace Greeley (New York: Harper & brothers, 1848), p. 203.

18. Filler, *Crusade Against Slavery*, p. 222.

19. John G. Fee, *An Anti-Slavery Manual* (Maysville, Ky.: Herald Office, 1848), pp. vi–vii.

20. Hinton R. Helper, *The Impending Crisis of the South: How to Meet It* (New York: Burdick Brothers, 1857), p. 41.

21. Filler, *Crusade Against Slavery*, p. 255; Hugh Talmage Lefler, "Hinton Rowan Helper: Advocate of a 'White America,'" in *Southern Sketches*, no. 1 (Charlottesville, Va.: Historical Publishing Co., 1935), pp. 6–7.

22. Helper, *Impending Crisis*, p. 24.

23. Allan Nevins, *The Emergence of Lincoln*, vol. 1, *Douglas, Buchanan, and Party Chaos 1857–1859* (New York: Charles Scribner's, 1950), p. 213; Avery O. Craven, *The Growth of Southern Nationalism, A History of the South*, vol. 6 (Baton Rouge, Louisiana State University Press, 1953), p. 251.

24. Filler, *Crusade Against Slavery*, p. 256; Hugh C. Bailey, *Hinton Rowan Helper: Abolitionist-Racist, Southern Historical Publications #7* (University, Ala., 1965), p. 83.

25. Samuel Wolfe, *Helper's Impending Crisis Dissected* (New York: J. T. Lloyd, 1860), pp. 42–43, 73.

26. *National Cyclopaedia of American Biography*, s.v. "Schade, Louis." After the Civil War, Schade was defense lawyer for ex-Confederate Captain Henry Wirz in the Andersonville Prison Trial.

27. Louis Schade, *A Book for the "Impending Crisis!" Appeal to the Common Sense and Patriotism of the People of the United States, "Helperism" Annihilated! The "Irrepressible Conflict" and Its Consequences* (Washington, D.C.: Little, Morris, 1860), pp. 56–57.

Chapter Five

1. Binkley, *Political Parties*, pp. 187–88.

2. Ibid., pp. 188–89.

3. Frank L. Mott, *A History of American Magazines 1741–1850* (New York: D. Appleton, 1930), pp. 750–53.

4. Seymour M. Lipset, and Earl Raab, *The Politics of Unreason: Right-Wing Extremism in America, 1790–1970* (New York: Harper & Row, 1970), pp. 58–59.

5. "Movements of the Enemy," *American Whig Review*, September 1852, p. 195.

6. Binkley, *Political Parties*, pp. 179–80; Filler, *Crusade Against Slavery*, p. 212.

7. Avery O. Craven, *Growth of Southern Nationalism*, pp. 128–41.

8. "The Foreign Policy of the Incoming Administration," *American Whig Review*, December 1852, p. 505.

9. Lipset and Raab, *The Politics of Unreason*, pp. 52–53.

10. *Dictionary of American Biography*, s.v. "Wilson, Henry," by George H. Haynes.

11. Henry Wilson, *History of the Rise and Fall of the Slave Power in America*, 9th ed., 3 vols. (Boston: Houghton, Mifflin, 1875–1877), 2:419.

12. *The Know-Nothing And American Crusader* (Boston), 25 September 1854.

13. Ibid.

14. Ibid.

15. *The Satanic Plot, or Awful Crimes of Popery in High and Low Places by a Know Nothing* (Boston: N. B. Parsons, 1855), p. 5.

16. Wilson, *Slave Power*, 2:422–33; Binkley, *Political Parties*, p. 195; Filler, *The Crusade Against Slavery*, p. 231.

17. Louis Schade, *The Immigration into the United States from a Statistical and National-Economical Point of View* (Washington, D.C.: Union Office, 1856), p. 12.

18. Roy F. Nichols, *The Disruption of American Democracy* (New York: Macmillan, 1948), pp. 42–43.

19. *Words of Counsel to Men of Business by a Man of Business* (n.p., n.d.), p. 10.

20. Mich. W. Cluskey, comp., *The Democratic Hand Book* (Washington, D.C.: R. A. Waters, 1856), p. 15.

21. Mich. W. Cluskey, ed., *Political Text-Book or Encyclopedia*, 12th ed. (Philadelphia: J. B. Smith & Co., 1860) s.v. "The Republican Association of Washington."

22. "The Late Election," *Putnam's Magazine*, December 1856, p. 647.

23. Python, "The Relative Political Status of the North and the South," *DeBow's Review*, February 1857, p. 114.

24. Python, "The Issues of 1860," *DeBow's Review*, March 1860, p. 245.

25. Cluskey, *Political Text-Book*, 12th ed., s.v. "Abolition Party."

26. *Biographical Directory of the American Congress 1774–1971*, s.v. "Florence, Thomas Birch"; *National Democratic Quarterly Review*, November 1859.

27. "The Relation of the Democratic Party to the Government of the United States," *Democratic Review*, November 1859, p. 4.

28. "Southern Wealth and Northern Profits," *Democratic Review*, June 1860, p. 403.

29. "John C. Breckinridge," *Democratic Review*, October 1860, p. 618.

30. *The Great Issue to be Decided in November Next! Shall the Constitution and the Union Stand or Fall, Shall Sectionalism Triumph? Lincoln and His Supporters.* [Democratic party (Southern) National Committee, 1860].

31. *New York Herald*, 20 July 1860, p. 4.

32. *New York Times*, 14 July 1860, p. 4.

33. *New York Herald*, 1 July 1860, p. 6.

34. George H. Mayer, *The Republican Party 1854–1964* (New York: Oxford University Press, 1964), p. 74; *New York Herald*, 27 October 1860, p. 6.

35. *New York Daily-Tribune*, 4 July 1860, p. 4.

36. Abraham Lincoln, *The Republican Party Vindicated—The Demands of the South Explained*, speech delivered at the Cooper Institute, New York City, 27 February 1860 (n.p.).

37. *Biographical Directory of the American Congress 1774–1971*, s.v. "Edgerton, Sidney."

38. Sidney Edgerton, *The Irrepressible Conflict,* speech delivered in the House of Representatives, 29 February 1860 (n.p.), p. 7.

39. *Biographical Directory of the American Congress 1774–1971,* s.v. "Duell, Rodolphus Holland," p. 883; R. H. Duell, *Position of Parties,* speech delivered in the House of Representatives, 12 April 1860 (n.p.), pp. 1–8.

40. Duell, *Position of Parties,* p. 2.

41. *New York Herald,* 8 November 1860, p. 4.

Chapter Six

1. "The Impending Fate of the Country," *DeBow's Review,* December 1866, p. 562.

2. E. L. Godkin, "The Essence of the Reconstruction Question," *Nation,* 4 July 1865, p. 4.

3. James S. Pike, *The Prostrate State: South Carolina Under Negro Government* (1874; reprint ed., New York: Loring & Mussey, 1935), pp. xv–xviii. Commager, who provided an introduction to the reprint, calls Pike's descriptions graphic, his criticisms just, his observations shrewd, and his conclusions sound (pp. xviii–xix).

4. John Wallace, *Carpetbag Rule in Florida: The Inside Workings of the Reconstruction of Civil Government in Florida after the Close of the Civil War* (1888; reprint ed., Gainesville: University of Florida Press, 1964), pp. xxii–xxiv, 3, 35–38.

5. Jerrell H. Shofner, *Nor Is It Over Yet: Florida in the Era of Reconstruction* (Gainesville: University of Florida Press, 1974), p. 76.

6. Wallace, *Carpetbag Days,* p. 324.

7. *Biographical Directory of the American Congress 1774–1971,* s.v. "Herbert, Hilary Abner"; Vernon Wharton, *"Reconstruction" in Writing Southern History: Essays in Historiography in Honor of Fletcher Green,* ed. Arthur S. Link and Rembert Patrick (Baton Rouge: Louisiana State University Press, 1967), p. 299.

8. Hilary A. Herbert et al., *Why the Solid South or Reconstruction and Its Results* (Baltimore: R. H. Woodward, 1890), p. 37.

9. E. Mertin Coulter, *A History of the South,* vol. 8, *The South During Reconstruction, 1865–1877* (Baton Rouge: Louisiana State University Press, 1947), pp. 36, 132, 386; John S. Ezell, *The South Since 1865* (New York: Macmillan, 1963); p. 96; Binkley, *Political Parties,* pp. 95–98; John A. Garraty, *The American Nation,* 2d ed. (New York: Harper & Row, 1971), pp. 161, 183–84.

10. Herbert Quick, "A Good Old Rebel," *Colliers,* 4 April 1914, pp. 20–21.

11. Mary Abigail Dodge (Gail Hamilton), *Biography of James G. Blaine* (Norwich, Conn.: Henry Publishing Company, 1895), pp. 324–25.

12. *Biographical Directory of the American Congress 1774–1971*, s.v. "Blaine, James Gillespie," "Hill, Benjamin Harvey."

13. Benjamin H. Hill, Jr., *Senator Benjamin H. Hill of Georgia, His Life, Speeches and Writings*, (Atlanta: T.H.P. Bloodworth, 1892), pp. 442–43, 460.

14. Joel Chandler Harris, *Life of Henry W. Grady including his Writings and Speeches* (New York: Cassell Publishing Company, 1890), p. 83.

15. Curti, *American Thought*, p. 485; Paul Gaston, *The New South Creed: A Study in Southern Mythmaking* (New York: Alfred A. Knopf, 1970), p. 85.

16. Gaston, *New South Creed*, p. 87; Harris, *Grady*, p. 66; Ezell, *South Since 1865*, p. 103.

17. Harris, *Grady*, pp. 85–86.

18. George W. Cable, "The Freedman's Case in Equity," *Century*, January 1885, p. 409.

19. Louis Rubin, *George W. Cable: The Life and Times of a Southern Heretic* (New York: Pegasus, 1969), p. 179.

20. Henry Grady, "In Plain Black and White," *Century*, April 1885, p. 909.

21. Rubin, *Cable*, p. 180.

22. Grady, "In Plain Black and White," p. 917.

23. Rubin, *Cable*, p. 181.

24. George W. Cable, *The Silent South: Together with the Freedman's Case in Equity and the Convict Lease System* (New York: Charles Scribner's, 1899), p. 53.

25. Frederick Douglass, *Why is the Negro Lynched?* (Bridgewater: John Whitby, 1895), p. 2.

26. Louis R. Harlan, *Booker T. Washington: The Making of a Black Leader* (New York: Oxford University Press, 1972), p. 204.

27. Booker T. Washington, *Up From Slavery: An Autobiography* (Garden City, N.Y.: Doubleday, Page, 1919), pp. 221–23.

28. Harlan, *Washington*, pp. 220–25.

29. W. E. Burghardt DuBois, *The Souls of Black Folk: Essays and Sketches*, 3d ed. (Chicago: A. C. McClurg, 1903), p. 50.

Chapter Seven

1. E. L. Godkin, *The Gilded Age Letters of E. L. Godkin*, ed. William M. Armstrong (Albany: University of New York Press, 1974), p. 30. See also Rollo Godkin, *Life and Letters of Edwin Lawrence Godkin*, 2 vols. (New York: Macmillan, 1907).

2. "The Great Festival," *Nation*, 4 July, 1865, p. 5.

3. E. L. Godkin, "The Negro's Claim to Office," *Nation*, 1 August 1867, p. 90.

4. E. L. Godkin, "The Indian Difficulty," *Nation*, 31 December 1868, pp. 544–45.

5. E. L. Godkin, "A Neglected Side of the Woman's Rights Question," *Nation*, 26 November 1868, pp. 434–35.

6. E. L. Godkin, "The Candidates Participation in the Canvass," *Nation*, 12 August 1880, p. 106.

7. E. L. Godkin, "Humanitarianism," *Nation*, 23 January 1868, p. 68.

8. Mayer, *Republican Party*, p. 173.

9. Grimes, *Political Thought*, p. 304.

10. Grimes, *Political Thought*, pp. 304–5; Beitzinger, *Political Thought*, pp. 420–22, Curti, *American Thought*, pp. 640–41.

11. Ibid., p. 302.

12. Beitzinger, *Political Thought*, p. 410.

13. William G. Sumner, *War and Other Essays*, ed. Albert G. Keller (New Haven: Yale University Press, 1911), p. xiv.

14. Sumner, *The Forgotten Man and Other Essays* (New Haven: Yale University Press, 1918), p. 10.

15. Sumner, *War and Other Essays*, p. 222.

16. Joseph F. Wall, *Andrew Carnegie* (New York: Oxford University Press, 1970), pp. 381, 392.

17. Wall, *Carnegie*, pp. 445–46; Robert G. McCloskey, *American Conservatism In The Age of Enterprise* (Cambridge: Harvard University Press, 1951), pp. 156–58.

18. Andrew Carnegie, *Triumphant Democracy or Fifty Years—March of the Republic* (1886; reprint ed., Garden City, N.Y.: Doubleday, Doran, 1933), p. 23. Henry Wirz, who commanded at the prison at Andersonville, was executed because of an emotional outburst of revenge. See Ovid L. Futch *History of Andersonville Prison* (Gainesville: University of Florida Press, 1968). "Jefferson Davis emerged from his voluntary plantation exile in 1886, when Henry Grady persuaded him to assist in repairing the political fortunes of Georgian General John B. Gordon. Davis' tour of the old Confederate South was described as triumphant." C. Vann Woodward, *A History of the South*, vol. 9, *Origins of the New South, 1877–1913* (Baton Rouge: Louisiana State University Press, 1951), p. 155.

19. Carnegie, *Triumphant Democracy*, p. 24.

20. Wall, *Carnegie*, pp. 805–6.

21. Andrew Carnegie, *The Gospel of Wealth and Other Timely Essays* (New York: Century, 1901), p. xxiii.

22. *National Cyclopaedia*, s.v. "Tucker, William Jewett."

23. William J. Tucker, "Gospel of Wealth," *Andover Review*, 15 (June 1891), 631–32.

24. McCloskey, *American Conservatism*, p. 147.

25. Carnegie, *Gospel of Wealth*, p. 144.

26. McCloskey, *American Conservatism*, p. 149; Wall, *Carnegie*, pp. 551–58.

27. William C. Oates, "The Homestead Strike: I. A Congressional View," *North American Review*, September 1892, pp. 355–61.

28. *Dictionary of American Biography*, s.v. "Curtis, George Ticknor," by Carl Russell Fish; *National Cyclopaedia*, s.v. "Curtis, George Ticknor";

George T. Curtis, "The Homestead Strike: II. A Constitutional View," *North American Review*, September 1892, pp. 364–70.

29. Curtis, "Constitutional View," p. 368.

30. T. V. Powderly, "The Homestead Strike: III. A Knight of Labor's View," *North American Review*, September, 1892, pp. 370–71.

31. Ibid., p. 373. Throughout his career Powderly opposed strikes and boycotts. Only after all other alternatives were exhausted did he support them. See Terrance V. Powderly, *The Path I Trod* (New York: Columbia University Press, 1940).

32. Edward R. Lewis, *A History of American Political Thought from the Civil War to the World War* (New York: Macmillan, 1937), p. 283.

33. Arthur E. Morgan, *Edward Bellamy*, Columbia Studies in American Culture, no. 15 (New York: Columbia University Press, 1944), pp. vi–vii.

34. Edward Bellamy, *Looking Backward: 2000–1887*, intro. Sylvester Baxter (Boston: Ticknor & Co., 1887).

35. Grimes, *American Political Thought*, p. 343.

36. Curti, *American Thought*, pp. 561–64; Grimes *Political Thought*, pp. 419–22; *Columbia Encyclopedia*, 3d ed. (1963), s.v. "pragmatism."

37. *Columbia Encyclopedia*, s.v. "pragmatism"; Beitzinger, *Political Thought*, pp. 469–76.

Chapter Eight

1. *Dictionary of American Biography*, s.v. "Weaver, James Baird," by John Donald Hicks.

2. Thomas H. McKee, *The National Conventions and Platforms of All Political Parties: 1789 to 1905. Convention, Popular and Electoral Vote* (1906; reprint ed., New York: Burt Franklin, 1971), pp. 278–79.

3. Binkley, *Political Parties*, p. 316.

4. James B. Weaver, *A Call to Action* (1892; reprint ed., New York: Arno Press, 1974), p. 394.

5. Mary E. Lease, *The Problem of Civilization Solved* (Chicago: Laird & Lee, 1895), pp. 267–68.

6. Thomas E. Watson, "Why the People's Party Should Elect the Next President," *Arena*, July 1892, pp. 201–4.

7. E. L. Godkin, "The Week," *Nation*, 7 July 1892, p. 1.

8. *Dictionary of American Biography*, s.v. "Lea, Henry Charles," by Dana C. Munro; Henry C. Lea, "The Duty of Political Independents," *Independent*, 20 October 1892, p. 1471.

9. *Dictionary of American Biography*, "Lea."

10. Lea, "Duty of Political Independents," p. 1471.

11. E. L. Godkin, "A Gigantic Bunco Game," *Nation*, 27 October 1892, p. 312.

12. *Dictionary of American Biography*, s.v. "Tanner, Benjamin T." by Harold G. Villard; *National Cyclopaedia*, s.v. "Tanner, Benjamin T."

13. Benjamin T. Tanner, "The Republican Defeat, A Negro's Explanation," *Independent*, 24 November 1892, p. 1659.

14. E. L. Godkin, "The Republican Tweedledum and the Democratic Tweedledee," *Nation*, 3 May 1894, p. 322.

15. Roswell G. Horr and William H. Harvey, *The Great Debate on the Financial Question between Hon. Roswell G. Horr of New York and William H. Harvey of Illinois* (Chicago: Debate Publishing Company, 1895), p. 3; Lewis, *American Political Thought*, p. 297.

16. Horr and Harvey, *Debate*, pp. 4–8.

17. Lewis, *American Political Thought*, p. 297.

18. Horr and Harvey, *Debate*, p. 229.

19. J. C. Long, *Bryan The Great Commoner* (New York: D. Appleton, 1928), pp. 67–68, 80–84.

20. Binkley, *Political Parties*, p. 320; Andrew D. White, "Encouragements in the Present Crisis," *Forum*, September 1896, pp. 16–17; *Columbia Encyclopedia*, 3 ed. (1963), s.v. "White, Andrew D."

21. White, "Present Crisis," pp. 16, 29.

22. Isaac L. Rice, "Thou Shalt Not Steal," *Forum*, September 1896, pp. 1, 10.

23. Louis W. Koenig, *Bryan: A Political Biography of William Jennings Bryan* (New York: G. P. Putnam's, 1971), pp. 240–41, 243, 246–47.

24. Ibid., pp. 251–54.

25. *Columbia Encyclopedia*, 3d ed. (1963), s.v. "Mahan, Alfred Thayer"; *Dictionary of American Biography*, s.v. "Mahan, Alfred Thayer," by Allan Westcott.

26. Alfred T. Mahan, *Mahan on Naval Warfare: Selections from the Writings of Rear Admiral Alfred T. Mahan*, ed. Allan Westcott (Boston: Little, Brown, 1918), p. 3.

27. Captain A. T. Mahan, "Effects of Asiatic Conditions Upon International Policies," *North American Review*, November 1900, pp. 609–10, 622.

28. John Braeman, *Albert J. Beveridge* (Chicago: University of Chicago Press, 1971), p. 5.

29. Braeman, *Beveridge*, pp. 5, 22–24.

30. Albert Beveridge, *For the Greater Republic, Not for Imperialism: An Address Delivered at the Union League of Philadelphia* (February 15, 1899), p. 3.

31. Braeman, *Beveridge*, pp. 24, 42.

32. Beveridge, *Greater Republic*, p. 10.

33. Edward Atkinson, "Jingoes and Silverites," *North American Review*, November 1895, pp. 554–55; *Dictionary of American Biography*, s.v. "Atkinson, Edward," by Roswell Cheney McCrea.

34. Atkinson, "Jingoes and Silverites," p. 555.

35. Horace N. Fisher, "The Development of Our Foreign Policy," *Atlantic Monthly*, October 1898, pp. 552–55.

36. Richard Olney, "Growth of Our Foreign Policy," *Atlantic Monthly*, March 1900, p. 289.

37. David D. Henry, *William Vaughn Moody: A Study* (1931; reprint ed., Folcroft, Pa.: Folcroft Library Editions, 1973), p. 51.

38. William V. Moody, *The Poems and Plays*, intro. John M. Manly, vol. 1 (Boston: Houghton Mifflin Co., 1900), pp. 15, 18–19, 23–25.

39. *Dictionary of American Biography*, s.v. "Nelson, Henry Loomis," by George B. Dutton; Henry L. Nelson, "The Political Horizon: I. The Development of Our Socialism," *Atlantic Monthly*, March 1900, pp. 309–22; Henry L. Nelson, "The Political Horizon: II. The Coming Campaign," *Atlantic Monthly*, April 1900, pp. 560–68.

40. Nelson, "Political Horizon: I," p. 309.

41. Nelson, "Political Horizon: II," p. 560.

Chapter Nine

1. Richard H. Pells, *Radical Visions and American Dreams: Culture and Social Thought in the Depression Years* (New York: Harper & Row, 1973), pp. 3–4, 30.

2. Edward A. Ross, *Sin and Society: An Analysis of Latter-Day Iniquity* (1907; reprint ed., Gloucester, Mass.: Peter Smith, 1965), p. 3.

3. Thorstein Veblen, *The Theory of the Leisure Class* (1899; reprint ed., New York: B. W. Huebsch, 1918), pp. 227–37; *The Portable Veblen*, ed. Max Lerner, (New York: Viking Press, 1948), pp. 33–36; David W. Noble, *The Paradox of Progressive Thought* (Minneapolis: University of Minnesota Press, 1958), pp. 199–200; Eric F. Goldman, *Rendezvous with Destiny* (1952; reprint ed., New York: Vintage, 1956), p. 90.

4. Herbert Croly, *The Promise of American Life* (1909; reprint ed., Hamden, Conn.: Archor Books, 1963), pp. 29–30, 43–44, 81; Henry F. May, *The End of American Innocence* (New York: Alfred A. Knopf, 1959), pp. 317–18.

5. Grimes, *Political Thought*, p. 390.

6. Arthur F. Bentley, *The Process of Government*, ed. Peter H. Odegard, (Cambridge, Mass.: Harvard University Press, 1967), pp. xxx–xxxi; Beitzinger, *Political Thought*, p. 500; Curti, *American Thought*, p. 573.

7. *Columbia Encyclopedia*, 3d ed. (1963), s.v. "Addams, Jane."

8. Jane Addams, *Twenty Years at Hull-House with Autobiographical Notes* (New York: Macmillan, 1929), p. 310.

9. *Columbia Encyclopedia*, 3d ed. (1963), s.v. "Riis, Jacob August"; Jacob A. Riis, *How the Other Half Lives: Studies Among the Tenements of New York* (New York: Charles Scribner's, 1904), p. 2.

10. S. S. McClure, "Editorial," *McClure's*, January 1903, p. 336. Separate Twayne series volumes cover two of the major muckrakers, Lincoln Steffens and Ida M. Tarbell.

11. C. C. Regier, *The Era of the Muckrakers* (1932; reprint ed., Gloucester, Mass.: Peter Smith, 1957), pp. 1–9; Arthur and Lila Weinberg, *The Muckrakers: The Era in Journalism that Moved America to Reform—The*

Most Significant Magazine Articles of 1902–1912 (New York: Simon and Schuster, 1961), pp. xvi–xvii, 58–65.

12. *Dictionary of American Biography*, s.v. "Phillips, David Graham," by Granville Hicks; *National Cyclopaedia of American Biography*, s.v. "Phillips, David Graham."

13. David Graham Phillips, "The Treason of the Senate," *Cosmopolitan*, March 1906, p. 487.

14. *Columbia Encyclopedia*, s.v. "Sinclair, Upton"; Regier, *Muckrakers*, pp. 134–35; Weinberg, *Muckrakers*, pp. 205–6.

15. Upton Sinclair, *The Jungle* (New York: Doubleday, Page, 1906), pp. 112–13.

16. Charles E. Russell, *The Greatest Trust in the World* (New York: Ridgway-Thayer, 1905), p. 1. This book consists of the articles which appeared in *Everybody's*.

17. J. Ogden Armour, *The Packers The Private Car Lines and the People* (Philadelphia: Henry Altemus, 1906), pp. 363.

18. Regier, *Muckrakers*, pp. 147–48.

19. Ray S. Baker, "The Right to Work," *McClure's*, January 1903, p. 323.

20. Ray S. Baker, "The Reign of Lawlessness: Anarchy and Despotism in Colorado," *McClure's*, May 1904, p. 43.

21. Ray S. Baker, "Organized Capital Challenges Organized Labor," *McClure's*, July 1904, p. 281.

22. Merrill A. Teague, "Bucket-Shop Sharks," *Everybody's*, June 1906, p. 735.

23. Regier, *Muckrakers*, p. 159.

24. Charles E. Russell, "The Tenements of Trinity Church," *Everybody's*, July 1908, p. 47.

25. George K. Turner, "The Daughters of the Poor," *McClure's*, November 1909, pp. 60–61.

26. Regier, *Muckrakers*, pp. 154–55; Ellery Sedgwick, "The Man with the Muck Rake," *American*, May 1906, pp. 111–12.

27. Sedgwick, "Muck Rake," p. 111.

Chapter Ten

1. Henry S. Commager, *The American Mind: An Interpretation of American Thought and Character Since the 1880's* (New Haven: Yale University Press, 1950), pp. 406–8: Curti, *American Thought*, p. 611.

2. Christopher Lasch, *The New Radicalism in America 1889–1963* (1965, reprint ed., New York: Vintage Press, 1967), pp. 69–71: Daniel Aaron, *Writers on the Left* (New York: Harcourt, Brace & World, 1961), pp. 1–29.

3. Aaron, *Writers on the Left*, pp. 45–48: Louis Filler, *Randolph Bourne* (1943; reprint ed., New York: Citadel Press, 1966), pp. 1–42: Lasch, *New Radicalism*, pp. 76–84.

4. Lasch, *New Radicalism*, p. 85.

5. Randolph Bourne, *The History of a Literary Radical* (New York: S. A. Russell, 1956), p. 193.

6. Bourne, *Literary Radical*, p. 210: Aaron, *Writers on the Left*, p. 66.

7. Aaron, *Writers on the Left*, pp. 37–41: Robert A. Rosenstone, *Romantic Revolutionary: A Biography of John Reed* (New York: Alfred A. Knopf, 1975), pp. 9, 117–32, 149–69, 356.

8. Charles Wellborn, *Twentieth Century Pilgrimage: Walter Lippmann and the Public Philosophy* (Baton Rouge: Louisiana State University Press, 1969), pp. 13, 18, 20, 25–29, 43, 177, 185: Gerald N. Grob and Robert N. Beck, eds., *American Ideas: Source Readings in the Intellectual History of the United States*, vol. 2, *Dilemmas of Maturity 1865–1962* (New York: Free Press, 1963), p. 380.

9. Lasch, *New Radicalism*, p. 178: George T. Blakey, *Historians on the Homefront: American Propagandists for the Great War* (Lexington, Ky.: University of Kentucky Press, 1970), pp. 16–17.

10. Henry L. Mencken, *Carnival of Buncombe*, ed. Malcolm Moos (Baltimore: Johns Hopkins University Press, 1956), p. 24. Quoted by permission of the publishers.

11. William Allen White, *Masks in a Pageant* (New York: Macmillan, 1928), p. 230.

12. William Allen White, *Forty Years on Main Street* (New York: Farrar & Rinehart, 1937), p. 158.

13. William Allen White, "William Allen White Sizes 'Em Up," *Colliers*, 9 August 1924, pp. 7–8, 27.

14. Will Rogers, *Convention Articles of Will Rogers*, ed. Joseph A. Stout, Jr. (Stillwater, Okla.: Oklahoma State University Press, 1976), pp. 6, 21.

15. Twelve Southerners, *I'll Take My Stand: The South and The Agrarian Tradition* (1930; reprint ed., New York: Harper Torchbooks, 1962), p. x.

16. John Crowe Ransome, "Reconstructed But Unregenerate," in *I'll Take My Stand*, pp. 7–10.

17. Frank L. Owsley, "The Irrepressible Conflict," in *I'll Take My Stand*, p. 74.

18. Allen Tate, "Remarks on the Southern Religion," in *I'll Take My Stand*, p. 166.

19. John Gould Fletcher, "Education Past and Present," in *I'll Take My Stand*, p. 117.

20. Clinton Rossiter, *Conservatism in America* (New York: Alfred A. Knopf, 1955), p. 154.

21. Grimes, *American Political Thought*, p. 407.

22. Herbert Hoover, *Addresses Upon the American Road: 1933–1938*. (New York: Charles Scribner's, 1938), pp. 1–5.

23. Charles A. Beard and George H. E. Smith, *The Future Comes: A Study of the New Deal* (New York: Macmillan, 1933), p. 165–66.

24. Franklin D. Roosevelt, *On Our Way* (New York: John Day, 1934), p. xi.

25. Louis Hartz, *The Liberal Tradition in America* (New York: Harcourt, Brace, 1955), p. 259.

26. Beard and Smith, *Future Comes*, pp. 169–70.

27. Rexford G. Tugwell, *The Battle for Democracy* (New York: 1935), p. 78.

28. Henry A. Wallace, "Talk at Great Lakes Exposition, Cleveland, Ohio, August 19, 1936," in *Democracy Reborn*, ed. Russell Lord (New York: Reynal & Hitchcock, 1944), p. 118.

29. Wallace, "Conclusion of the Weil Lectures, University of North Carolina, April 4, 1937," in *Democracy Reborn*, p. 123.

30. Harold L. Ickes, *The New Democracy* (New York: W. W. Norton, 1934), p. vii.

31. Hartz, *Liberal Tradition*, pp. 259–60.

32. Herbert Hoover, *The Challenge to Liberty* (New York: Charles Scribner's, 1934), pp. 104–6.

33. Herbert Hoover, *American Ideals versus The New Deal* (1936; reprint ed., St. Clair Shores, Mich.: Scholarly Press, 1972), p. 11.

34. S. Wells Utley, *The American System: Shall We Destroy It?* (Detroit: Speaker-Hines Press, 1936), p. 290.

35. James P. Warburg, *Hell Bent for Election* (New York: Doubleday, Doran, 1935), p. 2.

36. Norman Thomas, *After the New Deal, What?* (New York: Macmillan, 1936), pp. 8–12.

37. Earl Browder, *What Is Communism?* (New York: Vanguard Press, 1936), pp. 19, 22–28.

38. Huey Pierce Long, *My First Days in the White House* (Harrisburg, Pa.: Telegraph Press, 1935), p. 140.

39. Charles E. Coughlin, *A Series of Lectures on Social Justice* (Royal Oak, Mich.: The Radio League, 1935), p. 232.

40. Lawrence Dennis, *The Coming American Fascism* (1936; reprint ed., New York: AMS, 1972), pp. vii–ix, 296.

41. Henry L. Stimson, "The Decision to Use the Atomic Bomb," *Harper's*, February 1947, pp. 97–107.

42. Herbert Feis, *Japan Subdued: The Atomic Bomb and the End of the War in the Pacific* (Princeton: Princeton University Press, 1961), pp. 178–79, 186–87.

43. Hanson W. Baldwin, *Great Mistakes of the War* (New York: Harper, 1950), pp. 90–91, 102–7; *Commonweal*, 14 September 1945, p. 515.

44. Lloyd A. Free and Hadley Cantril, *The Political Belief of Americans: A Study of Public Opinion* (New Brunswick: Rutgers University Press, 1967), p. 5.

45. Rossiter, *Conservatism*, p. 186.

46. Ronald Lora, *Conservative Minds*, pp. 179–80.

47. Russell Kirk, *A Program for Conservatives* (Chicago: H. Regnery, 1954), pp. 5–10.

48. Peter Viereck, *Conservatism Revisited*, rev. ed. (New York: Collier Books, 1962), p. 21.

49. Lora, *Conservative Minds*, p. 191.

50. Gabriel, *Democratic Thought*, p. 435.

51. *Encyclopedia of American History*, rev. ed., ed. Richard B. Morris (New York: Harper & Row, 1965), p. 359.

52. Lora, *Conservative Minds*, pp. 195–97.

53. William F. Buckley, Jr. et al., *The Committee and Its Critics: A Calm Review of The House Committee on Un-American Activities* (New York: Putnam, 1962), p. 13.

54. Gabriel, *Democratic Thought*, pp. 437–39.

55. Commager, *The American Mind*, p. vii.

56. Hartz, *Liberal Tradition*, p. 300.

57. Lora, *Conservative Minds*, p. 230.

58. Schlesinger, *The Age of Jackson*, p. ix.

59. Lora, *Conservative Minds*, p. 132.

60. John K. Galbraith, *The Affluent Society* (Boston: Houghton Mifflin, 1958), p. 187–90.

61. Gunnar Myrdal, *An American Dilemma*, 2 vols. (1944; reprint ed., New York: McGraw-Hill, 1964).

62. *Brown et al.* v. *Board of Education of Topeka et al.* 347 U.S. 483 (1954).

63. C. Vann Woodward, *The Strange Career of Jim Crow*, 3d rev. ed. (New York: Oxford University Press, 1974), pp. 69, 169–71.

64. Robert Penn Warren, *Segregation: The Inner Conflict in the South* (New York: Vintage Books, 1956), pp. 3–109.

65. Willie Morris, *Yazoo* (New York: Harper's Magazine Press, 1971).

66. Howard Zinn, *The Southern Mystique* (1964; reprint ed., New York: Touchstone Books, 1972), pp. 262–63.

67. Martin L. King, *Why We Can't Wait* (1963; reprint ed., New York: Signet Books, 1964), pp. 76–95.

68. Stokely Carmichael and Charles Hamilton, *Black Power: The Politics of Liberation in America* (New York: Vintage Books, 1967), pp. 181–85.

69. James Baldwin, *Nobody Knows My Name* (New York: Dell, 1961), pp. 72–73.

70. Malcolm Little, *The Autobiography of Malcolm X* (1964; paperback ed., New York: Random House, 1966), p. xiii.

71. Carleton Putnam, *Race and Reason: A Yankee View* (Washington, D.C.: Public Affairs Press, 1961), pp. 6–9, 16, 164.

72. Peter A. Carmichael, *The South and Segregation* (Washington, D.C.: Public Affairs Press, 1965), pp. v–vi, 1–24, 80, 116–17, 175, 322.

73. Joe Azbell, *The Riotmakers* (Montgomery, Ala.: Oak Tree Books, 1968).

74. Putnam, *Race and Reason*, p. 72.

75. Irwin Unger, "The 'New Left' and American History: Some Recent Trends in United States Historiography," *American Historical Review* 72 (July 1967), 1237–43; Staughton Lynd, "The Origins of the New Left," in *Seasons of Rebellion: Protest and Radicalism in Recent America*, eds. Joseph Baskin and Robert A. Rosenstone (New York: Holt, Rinehart and Winston, 1972), pp. 119–30.

76. Robert Scheer and Warren Hinckle, "The 'Vietnam Lobby,'" in *A Vietnam Primer*, edited by editors of *Ramparts* (n.p., n.d.), p. 30.

77. *Southeast Asian Perspectives*, 1 (March 1971), back cover.

78. Lyndon Johnson, *The Vantage Point: Perspectives of the Presidency 1963–1969* (New York: Holt, Rinehart and Winston, 1971), pp. 117–19.

79. Frances Fitzgerald, *Fire in the Lake: The Vietnamese and the Americans in Vietnam* (Boston: Little, Brown, 1972), pp. 1–31, 442.

80. Bernard B. Fall, "This Isn't Munich, It's Spain," in *Viet Primer* (n.p., n.d.), pp. 68–69.

81. Wesley R. Fishel, "Three Brief Articles," in *Vietnam: Anatomy of a Conflict* (Itasca, Ill.: F. E. Peacock, 1968), p. 235.

82. Daniel Ellsberg, *Papers on the War* (New York: Simon and Schuster, 1972), pp. 35–39.

83. Arthur M. Schlesinger, Jr., *The Imperial Presidency* (Boston: Houghton Mifflin, 1973), p. 355.

84. Ellsberg, *Papers on the War*, pp. 33, 275–309.

85. Theodore White, *The Making of the President, 1960* (1961; reprint ed., New York: New American Library, 1967), pp. 64–73, 410–28.

86. Theodore Sorenson, *Kennedy* (New York: Harper & Row, 1965), pp. 11–42.

87. Arthur M. Schlesinger, Jr., *A Thousand Days* (Boston: Houghton Mifflin, 1965), p. 738.

88. Barry Goldwater, *The Conscience of a Conservative* (Shepherdsville, Ky.: Victor Publishing, 1960), pp. 9–123; G. W. Johnson, book review in *New Republic*, May 23, 1960, p. 20.

89. Tom Wicker, *JFK and LBJ: the influence of personality upon politics* (New York: William Morrow, 1968), pp. 148, 170–71, 182.

90. Sidney Hyman, *The Politics of Consensus* (New York: Random House, 1968), pp. 3–15, 31, 70–71.

91. Eric Goldman, *The Tragedy of Lyndon Johnson* (New York: Alfred A. Knopf, 1969), pp. 530–31.

92. Lewis Chester, Godfrey Hodgson, and Bruce Page, *An American Melodrama: The Presidential Campaign of 1968* (New York: Viking Press, 1969), p. 789.

93. Kevin P. Phillips, *The Emerging Republican Majority* (New Rochelle, N.Y.: Arlington House, 1969), pp. 461–74.

94. The Ripon Society, *The Lessons of Victory* (New York: Dial Press, 1969), preface.

95. Garry Wills, *Nixon Agonistes: The Crisis of the Self-Made Man* (Boston: Houghton Mifflin, 1970), pp. 3, 33, 79.

Chapter Eleven

1. Rossiter, *Conservatism in America*, p. 172.

Selected Bibliography

PRIMARY SOURCES

ADDAMS, JANE. *Twenty Years at Hull-House with Autobiographical Notes.* New York: Macmillan, 1929.

ARMOUR, J. OGDEN. *The Packers The Private Car Lines and the People.* Philadelphia: Henry Altemus, 1906.

American Whig Review, September–December 1852.

AMES, FISHER. "Intellect in a Democracy." In *The Prose Writers of America,* p. 99, edited by Rufus W. Griswold, 4th ed. Philadelphia: A. Hart, 1852.

————. *Works of Fisher Ames.* Boston: T. B. Wait, 1809.

ATKINSON, EDWARD. "Jingoes and Silverites." *North American Review,* November 1895, pp. 554–55.

AZBELL, JOE. *The Riotmakers.* Montgomery: Oak Tree Books, 1968.

BAKER, RAY STANNARD. "Organized Capital Challenges Organized Labor." *McClure's,* July 1904, pp. 279–92.

————. "The Reign of Lawlessness: Anarchy and Despotism in Colorado." *McClure's,* May 1904, pp. 43–46.

————. "The Right to Work." *McClure's,* January 1903, pp. 323–36.

BALDWIN, HANSON W. *Great Mistakes of the War.* New York: Harper, 1950.

BALDWIN, JAMES. *Nobody Knows My Name.* New York: Dell, 1961.

BELLAMY, EDWARD. *Looking Backward: 2000–1887.* Introduction by Sylvester Baxter. Boston: Ticknor & Co., 1887.

BENTLEY, ARTHUR F. *The Process of Government,* edited by Peter H. Odegard. Cambridge, Mass.: Harvard University Press, 1967.

BEVERIDGE, ALBERT. *For the Greater Republic, Not for Imperialism: An Address Delivered at the Union League of Philadelphia* (February 15, 1889). n.p., n.d.

BIRNEY, JAMES G. *A Letter on the Political Obligations of Abolitionists with a reply by William Lloyd Garrison.* Boston: Dow & Jackson, 1839.

BLAKEY, GEORGE T. *Historians on the Homefront: American Propagandists for the Great War.* Lexington, Ky.: University of Kentucky Press, 1970.

Boston Quarterly Review, January 1839, pp. 123–25.

BOURNE, RANDOLPH. *The History of a Literary Radical and Other Papers.* New York: S. A. Russell, 1956.

————. *The Radical Will: Selected Writings 1911–1918.* New York: Urizen Books, 1977.

BROWDER, EARL. *What Is Communism?* New York: Vanguard Press, 1936.

Brown et al. v. *Board of Education of Topeka et al.* 347 U.S. 483 (1954).

BUCKLEY, WILLIAM F. JR. et al. *The Committee and Its Critics: A Calm Review of the House Committee on Un-American Activities*. New York: Putnam, 1962.

CABLE, GEORGE W. "The Freedman's Case in Equity." *Century*, January 1885, pp. 409–18.

——. *The Silent South: Together with the Freedman's Case in Equity and the Convict Lease System*. New York: Charles Scribner's, 1899.

CALHOUN, JOHN C. "Speech on the Reception of Abolition Petitions, February, 1837," pp. 222–26, in *Speeches of John C. Calhoun. Delivered in the Congress of the United States from 1811 to the Present Time*. New York: Harper, 1843.

CAREY, MATHEW. *Addresses of the Philadelphia Society for the Promotion of National Industry*. 6th ed. Philadelphia, 1822.

——. *The New Olive Branch: or, An Attempt to Establish an Identity of Interest Between Agriculture, Manufactures, and Commerce; And to Prove that a Large Portion of the Manufacturing Industry of this Nation Has Been Sacrificed to Commerce; And That Commerce Has Suffered By this Policy Nearly As Much As Manufactures*. Philadelphia: M. Carey & Son, 1820.

——. *The Olive Branch; or, Faults on Both Sides, Federal and Democratic A Serious Appeal on the Necessity of Mutual Forgiveness and Harmony*. 7th ed. Philadelphia: M. Carey, 1815.

CARMICHAEL, PETER A. *The South and Segregation*. Washington, D.C.: Public Affairs Press, 1965.

CARMICHAEL, STOKELY, and HAMILTON, CHARLES. *Black Power: The Politics of Liberation in America*. New York: Vintage Books, 1967.

CARNEGIE, ANDREW. *The Gospel of Wealth and Other Timely Essays*. New York: Century, 1901.

——. *Triumphant Democracy; or Fifty Years' March of the Republic*. 1886; reprint ed., Garden City, N.Y.: Doubleday, Doran, 1933.

CHANNING, WILLIAM E. *The Works of William E. Channing, D. D*. Vol. 2. Boston: James Munroe, 1841.

CHESTER, LEWIS, HODGSON, GODFREY, and PAGE, BRUCE. *An American Melodrama: The Presidential Campaign of 1968*. New York: Viking Press, 1969.

CLAY, CASSIUS M. *The Writings of Cassius Marcellus Clay Including Speeches and Addresses*. Edited with preface and memoir by Horace Greeley. New York: Harper & brothers, 1848.

CLUSKEY, MICH. W., comp. *The Democratic Hand-Book*. Washington, D.C.: R. A. Waters, 1856.

——, ed. *Political Text-Book, or Encyclopedia*. 12th ed. Philadelphia: Jas. B. Smith, 1860.

COBBETT, WILLIAM. *Porcupine's Works; Containing Various Writings and Selections, Exhibiting a Faithful Picture of the United States of America*. London: Printed for Cobbett and Morgan, 1801.

Commonweal 14 September 1945, p. 515.

COUGHLIN, CHARLES E. *A Series of Lectures on Social Justice*, Royal Oak, Mich.: The Radio League of the Little Flower, 1935.

CROCKETT, DAVID. *An Account of Col. Crockett's Tour to the North and Down East, in the year of our Lord one thousand eight hundred and thirty four.* Philadelphia: E. L. Carey and A. Hart, 1835.

————. *Col. Crockett's Exploits and Adventures in Texas.* Philadelphia: T. K. and P. G. Collins, 1836.

————. *The Life of Martin Van Buren.* 10th ed. Philadelphia: Robert Wright, 1836.

CROLY, HERBERT. *The Promise of American Life.* 1909; reprint ed., Hamden, Conn.: Archor Books, 1963.

CURTIS, GEORGE T. "The Homestead Strike: II. A Constitutional View." *North American Review*, September 1892, pp. 364–70.

DENNIS, LAWRENCE. *The Coming American Fascism.* 1936; reprint ed., New York: AMS, 1972.

DEW, THOMAS R. *An Essay on Slavery.* Richmond: J. W. Randolph, 1849.

DODGE, MARY ABIGAIL (GAIL HAMILTON). *Biography of James G. Blaine.* Norwich, Conn.: Henry Publishing Company, 1895.

DOUGLASS, FREDERICK. *Oration, Delivered in Corinthian Hall, Rochester, July 4th, 1852.* Rochester: Lee, Mann, 1852.

————. *Why is the Negro Lynched?* Bridgewater: John Whitby, 1895. Reprint of article in *A.M.E. Church Review.*

DUBOIS, W. E. BURGHARDT. *The Souls of Black Folk: Essays and Sketches.* 3d ed. Chicago: A. C. McClurg, 1903.

DUELL, R. H. *Position of Parties.* Speech Delivered in the House of Representatives, 29 February 1860 (n.p.).

EDGERTON, SIDNEY. *The Irrepressible Conflict.* Speech Delivered in the House of Representatives, *Feb. 29, 1860.* n.p. n.d.

ELLSBERG, DANIEL. *Papers on the War.* New York: Simon and Schuster, 1972.

FALL, BERNARD B. *"This Isn't Munich, It's Spain."* In *A Viet Primer*, pp. 58–69. Edited by the editors of *Ramparts.* n.p., n.d.

FEE, JOHN G. *An Anti-Slavery Manual.* Maysville, Ky.: Herald office, 1848.

FEIS, HERBERT. *Japan Subdued: The Atomic Bomb and the End of the War in the Pacific.* Princeton: Princeton University Press, 1961.

FISHEL, WESLEY R. "Three Brief Articles." *In Vietnam: Anatomy of a Conflict*, edited by Wesley R. Fishel, pp. 220–35. Itasca, Ill.: F. E. Peacock, 1968.

FISHER, HORACE N. "The Development of Our Foreign Policy." *Atlantic Monthly*, October 1898, pp. 552–59.

FITZGERALD, FRANCES. *Fire in the Lake: The Vietnamese and the Americans in Vietnam.* Boston: Little, Brown, 1972.

FITZHUGH, GEORGE. *Cannibals All! or Slaves Without Masters.* Richmond: A. Morris, 1857.

FORD, PAUL LEICESTER, ed. *The Writings of Thomas Jefferson.* 10 Vols. New York: G. P. Putnam's, 1892–1899.

"The Foreign Policy of the Incoming Administration." *American Whig Review*, December 1852, pp. 505–11.

GALBRAITH, JOHN K. *The Affluent Society.* Boston: Houghton Mifflin, 1958.

GARLAND, HUGH A. *An Oration, Pronounced in Castle Garden, July 27, 1840, in Celebration of the Second Declaration of Independence, or the Passage of the Independent Treasury Bill.* New York: William G. Boggs, 1840.

GODKIN, E. L. "The Candidates Participation in the Canvass." *Nation*, 12 August 1880, p. 106.

———. "The Essence of the Reconstruction Question." *Nation*, 4 July 1865, pp. 4–5.

———. "A Gigantic Bunco Game." *Nation*, 27 October 1892, p. 312.

———. *The Gilded Age Letters of E. L. Godkin.* Edited by William M. Armstrong. Albany: University of New York Press, 1974.

———. "Humanitarianism." *Nation*, 23 January 1868, p. 68.

———. "The Indian Difficulty." *Nation*, 31 December 1868, pp. 544–45.

———. "A Neglected Side of the Woman's Rights Question." *Nation*, 26 November 1868, pp. 434–35.

———. "The Negro's Claim to Office." *Nation*, 1 August 1867, p. 90.

———. "The Republican Tweedledum and the Democratic Tweedledee." *Nation*, 3 May 1884, p. 322.

———. "The Week." *Nation*, 7 July 1892, pp. 1–3.

GOLDMAN, ERIC F. *The Tragedy of Lyndon Johnson.* New York: Alfred A. Knopf, 1969.

GOLDWATER, BARRY. *The Conscience of a Conservative.* Shepherdsville, Ky.: Victor Publishing, 1960.

GOODELL, WILLIAM. *Slavery and Anti-Slavery; A History of the Great Struggle in Both Hemispheres; with a View of the Slavery Question in the United States.* New York: William Harned, 1852.

GRADY, HENRY. "In Plain Black and White." *Century*, April 1885, pp. 909–17.

GRAYSON, WILLIAM J. *The Hireling and the Slave, Chicora, and Other Poems.* Charleston: McCarter, 1856.

"The Great Festival." *Nation*, 1 August 1865, p. 5.

The Great Issue to Be Decided in November Next! Shall the Constitution and the Union Stand or Fall, Shall Sectionalism Triumph? Lincoln and His Supporters. [Democratic party (Southern) National Committee, 1860, n.p., n.d.].

GRISWOLD, RUFUS WILMOT. *The Prose Writers of America.* 4th ed., rev. Philadelphia: A. Hart, 1852.

HALBERSTAM, DAVID. *The Best and the Brightest.* New York: Random House, 1969.

———. *The Making of a Quagmine.* New York: Random House, 1964.

HAZARD, T. R. *Facts for the Laboring Man by a Laboring Man.* Newport, R.I.: James Atkinson, 1840.

HELPER, HINTON R. *The Impending Crisis of the South: How to Meet It.* New York: Burdick Brothers, 1857.

HERBERT, HILARY A. et al. *Why the Solid South or Reconstruction and Its Results.* Baltimore: R. H. Woodward, 1890.

HILL, BENJAMIN H., JR. *Senator Benjamin H. Hill of Georgia. His Life, Speeches and Writings.* Atlanta: T. H. P. Bloodworth & Co., 1892.

HOOVER, HERBERT T. *Addresses Upon the American Road: 1933–1938.* New York: Charles Scribner's, 1938.

———. *American Ideals versus the New Deal.* 1936; reprint ed., St. Clair Shores, Mich.: Scholarly Press, 1972.

———. *The Challenge to Liberty.* New York: Charles Scribner's, 1934.

HORR, ROSWELL G., and HARVEY, WILLIAM H. *The Great Debate on the Financial Question between Hon. Roswell G. Horr of New York and William H. Harvey of Illinois.* Chicago: Debate Publishing Company, 1895.

HUNT, COLONEL BENJ. FANEUIL. *Speech of Col. Benj. Faneuil Hunt of Charleston, South Carolina, Delivered at the Request of the Democratic Republican General Committee at the Mass Meeting of the Mechanics and Working Men of New York, in Reply to the Doctrines of Daniel Webster on the Currency and a National Bank.* New York: James Rees, 1840.

HYMAN, SIDNEY. *The Politics of Consensus.* New York: Random House, 1968.

ICKES, HAROLD L. *The New Democracy.* New York: W. W. Norton, 1934.

"The Impending Fate of the Country." *DeBow's Review,* December 1866, pp. 561–70.

JEFFERSON, THOMAS. *The Portable Thomas Jefferson,* edited by Merrill Peterson. New York: Viking Press, 1975.

"John C. Breckinridge." *National Democratic Quarterly Review,* October 1860, pp. 607–19.

JOHNSON, LYNDON BAINES. *The Vantage Point: Perspectives of the Presidency 1963–1969.* New York: Holt, Rinehart and Winston, 1971.

KING, MARTIN LUTHER, JR. *Stride Toward Freedom.* 1958; reprint ed., New York: Perennial Library 1964.

——— *Why We Can't Wait.* 1963; reprint ed., New York: Signet Books, 1964.

KIRK, RUSSELL. *A Program for Conservatives.* Chicago: H. Regnery, 1954.

The Know-Nothing And American Crusader (Boston), 25 September 1854.

"The Late Election." *Putnam's Magazine,* December 1856, pp. 647–54.

LEA, HENRY C. "The Duty of Political Independents." *Independent,* 20 October 1892, p. 1471.

LEASE, MARY E. *The Problem of Civilization Solved.* Chicago: Laird & Lee, 1895.

LEGGETT, WILLIAM. *A Collection of the Political Writings of William Leggett.* Selected and arranged with a preface by Theodore Sedgwick,

Jr. 2 Vols. New York: Taylor & Dodd, 1840.

The Liberator (Boston), 1 January 1831.

LINCOLN, ABRAHAM. *The Republican Party Vindicated—The Demands of the South Explained.* Speech at the Cooper Institute, New York City, 27 February 1860. n.p.

LITTLE, MALCOLM. *The Autobiography of Malcolm X.* 1964; paperback ed., New York: Random House, 1966.

LONG, HUEY PIERCE. *My First Days in the White House.* Harrisburg, Pa.: Telegraph Press, 1935.

LYND, STAUGHTON. "The Origins of the New Left." In *Seasons of Rebellion: Protest and Radicalism in Recent America*, edited by Joseph Boskin and Robert A. Rosenstone, pp. 119–30. New York: Holt, Rinehart and Winston, 1972.

McCLURE, S. S. "Editorial." *McClure's*, January 1903, p. 336.

McCulloch v. *Maryland* (1819) 4 Wheaton (W.S.) 316.

McKEE, THOMAS H. *The National Conventions and Platforms of All Political Parties: 1789 to 1905. Convention, Popular and Electoral Vote.* 1906; reprint ed., New York: Burt Franklin, 1971.

MAHAN, CAPTAIN A. T. "Effects of Asiatic Conditions Upon International Policies." *North American Review*, November 1900, pp. 609–26.

———. *Mahan on Naval Warfare: Selections from the Writings of Rear Admiral Alfred T. Mahan*, edited by Allan Westcott. Boston: Little, Brown, 1918.

MAYO, ROBERT. *Political Sketches of Eight Years in Washington.* Baltimore: Fielding Lucas, 1839.

MENCKEN, HENRY L. *A Carnival of Buncombe*, edited by Malcolm Moos. Baltimore: Johns Hopkins University, 1956.

MOODY, WILLIAM V. *The Poems and Plays*, introduction by John M. Manly. 2 Vols. Boston: Houghton Mifflin Co., 1900.

MORRIS, WILLIE. *Yazoo.* New York: Harper's Magazine Press, 1971.

MYRDAL, GUNNER. *An American Dilemma.* 2 Vols. 1944; reprint ed., New York: McGraw-Hill, 1964.

NELSON, HENRY L. "The Political Horizon: I. The Development of Our Socialism." *Atlantic Monthly*, March 1900, pp. 309–22.

———. "The Political Horizon: II. The Coming Campaign." *Atlantic Monthly*, April 1900, pp. 560–68.

New York Daily-Tribune, 1860.

New York Herald, 1860.

New York Times, 1860.

OATES, WILLIAM C. "The Homestead Strike: I. A Congressional View." *North American Review*, September 1892, pp. 355–64.

OLNEY, RICHARD. "Growth of Our Foreign Policy." *Atlantic Monthly*, March 1900, pp. 289–301.

PHILLIPS, DAVID GRAHAM. "The Treason of the Senate." *Cosmopolitan*, March 1906, pp. 487–501.

PHILLIPS, KEVIN P. *The Emerging Republican Majority.* New Rochelle, N.Y.: Arlington House, 1969.

PIKE, JAMES SHEPHERD. *The Prostrate State: South Carolina Under Negro Government.* 1874; reprint ed., New York: Loring & Mussey, 1935.

Political Mirror or Review of Jacksonism. New York: J. P. Peaslee, 1835.

Port Folio 3 (April 23, 1803).

POWDERLY, T. V. "The Homestead Strike: III. A Knight of Labor's View." *North American Review*, September 1892, pp. 370–75.

———. *The Path I Trod.* New York: Columbia University Press, 1940.

The Pro-Slavery Argument as Maintained by the Most Distinguished Writers of the Southern States, Containing the Several Essays, on the Subject, of Chancellor Harper, Governor Hammond, Dr. Simms, and Professor Dew. Charleston: Walker, Richards & Co., 1852.

PUTNAM, CARLETON. *Race and Reason: A Yankee View.* Washington: Public Affairs Press, 1961.

PYTHON. "The Issues of 1860," *DeBow's Review*, March 1860, pp. 245–72.

———. "The Relative Political Status of the North and the South," *DeBow's Review*, February 1857, pp. 113–32.

QUICK, HERBERT. "A Good Old Rebel." *Colliers*, 4 April 1914, pp. 20–21.

"The Relation of the Democratic Party to the Government of the United States." *National Democratic Quarterly Review*, November 1859, pp. 4–18.

RICE, ISAAC L. "Thou Shalt Not Steal." *Forum*, September 1896, pp. 1–15.

RIIS, JACOB A. *How the Other Half Lives: Studies Among the Tenements of New York.* New York: Charles Scribner's, 1904.

THE RIPON SOCIETY. *The Lessons of Victory.* New York: Dial Press, 1969.

ROGERS, WILL. *Convention Articles of Will Rogers.* Edited by Joseph A. Stout, Jr. Stillwater, Okla.: Oklahoma State University Press, 1976.

ROOSEVELT, FRANKLIN D. *On Our Way.* New York: John Day, 1934.

ROSS, EDWARD A. *Sin and Society: An Analysis of Latter-Day Iniquity.* 1907; reprint ed., Gloucester, Mass.: Peter Smith, 1965.

RUSSELL, CHARLES E. *The Greatest Trust in the World.* New York: Ridgway-Thayer, 1905.

———. "The Tenements of Trinity Church." *Everybody's*, July 1908, pp. 47–57.

The Satanic Plot, or Awful Crimes of Popery in High and Low Places by a Know Nothing. Boston: N. B. Parsons, 1855.

SCHADE, LOUIS, *A Book for the "Impending Crisis!" Appeal to the Common Sense and Patriotism of the People of the United States. "Helperism" Annihilated! The "Irrepressible Conflict" and Its Consequences.* Washington, D.C.: Little, Morris, 1860.

———. *The Immigration Into the United States of America, from a Statistical and National-Economical Point of View.* Washington, D.C.: Union Office, 1856.

SCHEER, ROBERT, and HINCKLE, WARREN. "The Vietnam Lobby." In *A Vietnam Primer*, pp. 23–36. Edited by the editors of *Ramparts*. n.p., n.d.

SCHLESINGER, ARTHUR M., JR. *A Thousand Days: John F. Kennedy in the White House.* Boston: Houghton Mifflin, 1965.

SEDGWICK, ELLERY. "The Man with the Muck Rake." *American*, May 1906, pp. 111–12.

SINCLAIR, UPTON. *The Jungle*. New York: Doubleday, Page, 1906.

SORENSON, THEODORE. *Kennedy*. New York: Harper & Row, 1965.

Southeast Asian Perspectives 1 (March 1971).

"Southern Wealth and Northern Profits." *National Democratic Quarterly Review*, June 1860, pp. 398–401.

SPOONER, LYSANDER. *The Unconstitutionality of Slavery*. Boston: Bela Marsh, 1845.

STIMSON, HENRY L. "The Decision to Use The Atomic Bomb." *Harper's*, February 1947, pp. 97–107.

SUMNER, WILLIAM G. *The Forgotten Man and Other Essays*. Edited by Albert G. Keller. New Haven: Yale University Press, 1918.

———. *War and Other Essays*. Edited by Albert G. Keller. New Haven: Yale University Press, 1911.

TANNER, BENJAMIN T. "The Republican Defeat: A Negro's Explanation." *Independent*, November 24, 1892, pp. 1658–59.

TAYLOR, JOHN. *Arator: Being a Series of Agricultural Essays, Practical and Political*. Petersburg: Whitworth & Yancey, 1818.

———. *An Inquiry into The Principles and Policy of the Government of the United States*. Fredericksburg: Green and Cady, 1814.

TEAGUE, MERRILL A. "Bucket-Shop Sharks." *Everybody's*, June 1906, pp. 723–35.

THOMAS, NORMAN. *After the New Deal, What?* New York: Macmillan, 1936.

The Trustees of Dartmouth College v. *Woodward* (1819) 4 Wheaton (U.S.) 581.

TUCKER, WILLIAM J. "The Gospel of Wealth." *Andover Review*, 15 (June, 1891), 631–45.

TUGWELL, REXFORD G. *The Battle for Democracy*. New York: Columbia University Press, 1935.

TURNER, GEORGE K. "The Daughters of the Poor." *McClure's*, November 1909, pp. 45–61.

TWELVE SOUTHERNERS. *I'll Take My Stand: The South and the Agrarian Tradition*. 1930; reprint ed., New York: Harper Torchbooks, 1962.

UTLEY, S. WELLS. *The American System: Shall We Destroy It?* Detroit: Speaker-Hines Press, 1936.

VEBLEN, THORSTEIN. *The Portable Veblen*. Edited by Max Lerner. New York: Viking Press, 1948.

——— *The Theory of the Leisure Class*. 1899; reprint ed., New York: B. W. Huebsch, 1922.

VIERECK, PETER. *Conservatism Revisited*. Rev. ed. New York: Collier Books, 1962.

WALLACE, HENRY. *Democracy Reborn*. Edited by Russell Lord. New York: Reynal & Hitchcock, 1944.

WALLACE, JOHN. *Carpetbag Rule in Florida: The Inside Workings of the Reconstruction of Civil Government in Florida after the Close of the*

Civil War. 1888; reprint ed., Gainesville: University of Florida Press, 1964.

WARBURG, JAMES P. *Hell Bent for Election.* Garden City, N.Y.: Doubleday, Doran, 1935.

WARREN, ROBERT PENN. *Segregation: The Inner Conflict in the South.* New York: Vintage Books, 1956.

WASHINGTON, BOOKER T. *Up from Slavery: An Autobiography.* Garden City, N.Y.: Doubleday, Page, 1919.

WATSON, THOMAS E. "Why the People's Party Should Elect the Next President." *Arena*, July 1892, pp. 201–4.

WEAVER, JAMES B. *A Call to Action.* 1892; reprint ed., New York: Arno Press, 1974.

WHITE, ANDREW D. "Encouragements in the Present Crisis." *Forum*, September 1896, pp. 16–30.

WHITE, THEODORE H. *The Making of the President 1960.* 1961; reprint ed., New York: New American Library, 1967.

WHITE, WILLIAM ALLEN. *Forty Years on Main Street.* New York: Farrar & Rinehart, 1937.

———. *Mask in a Pageant.* New York: Macmillan, 1928.

———. "William Allen White Sizes 'Em Up," *Colliers*, 9 August 1924, pp. 7–8, 27.

WICKER, TOM. *JFK and LBJ: the Influence of Personality Upon Politics.* New York: William Morrow, 1968.

WILLS, GARRY. *Nixon Agonistes: The Crisis of the Self-Made Man.* Boston: Houghton Mifflin, 1970.

WILSON, HENRY. *History of the Rise and Fall of the Slave Power in America.* 9th ed. 3 Vols. Boston: Houghton, Mifflin, 1875–1877.

WOLFE, SAMUEL. *Helper's Impending Crisis Dissected.* New York: J. T. Lloyd, 1860.

WOODWARD, C. VANN. *The Strange Career of Jim Crow.* 3d rev. ed. New York: Oxford University Press, 1974.

Words of Counsel to Men of Business by a Man of Business. N.p., n.d.

ZINN, HOWARD. *The Southern Mystique.* 1964; reprint ed., New York: Touchstone Books, 1972.

SECONDARY SOURCES

AARON, DANIEL. *Writers on the Left.* New York: Harcourt, Brace & World, 1961.

ABERNATHY, THOMAS P. *From Frontier to Plantation in Tennessee.* Southern Historical Publications no. 12. University, Ala.: University of Alabama Press, 1967.

BEARD, CHARLES A., and SMITH, GEORGE H. E. *The Future Comes: A Study of the New Deal.* New York: Macmillan, 1933.

BINKLEY, WILFRED. *American Political Parties: Their Natural History.* 4th ed. New York: Alfred A. Knopf, 1962.

Biographical Directory of the American Congress 1774–1971. Washington, D.C.: Government Printing Office, 1971.

BRAEMAN, JOHN. *Albert J. Beveridge.* Chicago: University of Chicago Press, 1971.

Columbia Encyclopedia, 3d ed. (1963).

COMMAGER, HENRY S. *The American Mind: An Interpretation of American Thoughts and Character Since the 1880's.* New Haven: Yale University Press, 1950.

COULTER, E. MERTON. *A History of the South.* Vol. 8. *The South During Reconstruction, 1865–1877.* Baton Rouge: Louisiana State University Press, 1947.

CRAVEN, AVERY O. *A History of the South.* Vol. 6. *The Growth of Southern Nationalism.* Baton Rouge: Louisiana State University Press, 1947.

CURTI, MERLE. *The Growth of American Thought.* 2d ed. New York: Harper & Row, 1951.

DAUER, MANNING J., and HAMMOND, HANS. "John Taylor: Democrat or Aristocrat." *The Journal of Politics* 6 (November, 1944): 381–403.

Dictionary of American Biography. Edited by Allen Johnson and Dumas Malone. New York: Charles Scribner's Sons, 1936.

Encyclopedia of American History. rev. ed. Edited by Richard B. Morris. New York: Harper & Row, 1965.

EZELL, JOHN S. *The South Since 1865.* New York: Macmillan, 1963.

FILLER, LOUIS. *Crusade Against Slavery.* New York: Harper, 1960.

———. *Randolph Bourne.* 1943; reprint ed., New York: Citadel Press, 1966.

FREE, LLOYD A., and CANTRIL, HADLEY. *The Political Belief of Americans: A Study of Public Opinion.* New Brunswick: Rutgers University Press, 1967.

FUTCH, OVID L. *History of Andersonville.* Gainesville: University of Florida Press, 1968.

GABRIEL, RALPH H. *The Course of American Democratic Thought.* 2d ed. New York: Ronald Press, 1956.

GARRATY, JOHN A. *The American Nation.* 2d ed. New York: Harper & Row, 1971.

GASTON, PAUL M. *The New South Creed: A Study in Southern Mythmaking.* New York: Alfred A. Knopf, 1970.

GODKIN, ROLLO. *Life and Letters of Edwin Lawrence Godkin.* 2 vols. New York: Macmillan, 1907.

GRIMES, ALAN P. *American Political Thought.* Rev. ed. New York: Holt, Rinehart and Winston, 1960.

GROB, GERALD N., and BECK, ROBERT N., eds. *American Ideas: Source Readings in the Intellectual History of the United States.* Vol. 2. *Dilemmas of Maturity 1865–1962,* New York: Free Press, 1963.

HARLAN, LOUIS R. *Booker T. Washington: The Making of a Black Leader.* New York: Oxford University Press, 1972.

HARRIS, JOEL CHANDLER. *Life of Henry W. Grady including His Writings and Speeches.* New York: Cassell Publishing Company, 1890.

HART, LOUIS. *The Liberal Tradition in America.* New York: Harcourt, Brace, 1955.

HENRY, DAVID D. *William Vaughn Moody: A Study.* 1931; reprint ed., Folcroft, Pa.: Folcroft Library Editions, 1973.

JOHNSON, G. W. Book review in *New Republic*, 23 May 1960, p. 20.

KOENIG, LOUIS, W. *Bryan: A Political Biography of William Jennings Bryan.* New York: G. P. Putnam's, 1971.

LASCH, CHRISTOPHER. *The New Radicalism in America 1889–1963.* 1965; reprint ed., New York: Vintage Books, 1967.

LEFLER, HUGH TALMAGE. "Hinton Rowan Helper Advocate of a 'White America'" in *Southern Sketches*, no. 1. Charlottesville, Va.: Historical Publishing Co., 1935, pp. 6–7.

LEWIS, EDWARD R. *A History of American Political Thought from the Civil War to the World War.* New York: Macmillan, 1937.

LIPSET, SEYMOUR M., and RAAB, EARL. *The Politics of Unreason: Right-Wing Extremism in America, 1790–1970.* New York: Harper & Row, 1970.

LLOYD, ARTHUR L. *The Slavery Controversy: 1831–1860.* Chapel Hill: University of North Carolina Press, 1939.

LONG, J. C. *Bryan the Great Commoner.* New York: D. Appleton, 1928.

LORA, RONALD. *Conservative Minds in America.* Chicago: Rand McNally, 1971.

McCLOSKEY, ROBERT G. *American Conservatism In the Age of Enterprise.* Cambridge: Harvard University Press, 1951.

MAY, HENRY F. *The End of American Innocence: A Study of the First Years of Our Own Time 1912–1917.* New York: Alfred A. Knopf, 1959.

MAYER, GEORGE H. *The Republican Party 1854–1964.* New York: Oxford University Press, 1964.

MILLER, PERRY. *The Life of the Mind in America from the Revolution to the Civil War.* New York: Harcourt, Brace & World, 1965.

MORGAN, ARTHUR E. *Edward Bellamy.* Columbia Studies in American Culture, no. 15. New York: Columbia University Press, 1944.

MOTT, FRANK LUTHER. *A History of American Magazines 1741–1850.* New York: D. Appleton, 1930.

National Cyclopaedia of American Biography. New York: James T. White, 1931.

NEVINS, ALLAN. *The Emergence of Lincoln.* Vol. 1. *Douglas, Buchanan, and Party Chaos 1857–1859.* New York: Charles Scribner's, 1950.

NOBLE, DAVID W. *The Paradox of Progressive Thought.* Minneapolis: University of Minnesota Press, 1958.

NICHOLS, ROY F. *The Disruption of American Democracy.* New York: Macmillan, 1948.

PARRINGTON, VERNON LOUIS. *Main Currents in American Thought.* Vol. 2. *1800–1860: The Romantic Revolution in America.* New York: Harcourt Brace, 1927.

PELLS, RICHARD H. *Radical Visions and American Dreams: Culture and Social Thought in The Depression Years.* New York: Harper & Row, 1973.

REGIER, C. C. *The Era of the Muckrakers.* 1932; reprint ed., Gloucester, Mass.: Peter Smith, 1957.

ROSENSTONE, ROBERT A. *Romantic Revolutionary: A Biography of John Reed.* New York: Alfred A. Knopf, 1975.

ROSSITER, CLINTON. *Conservatism in America.* New York: Alfred A. Knopf, 1955.

RUBIN, LOUIS D. *George W. Cable: The Life and Times of a Southern Heretic.* New York: Pegasus, 1969.

SCHLESINGER, ARTHUR M. *The Age of Jackson.* Boston: Little, Brown, 1946.
———. *The Imperial Presidency.* Boston: Houghton Mifflin, 1973.

SHOFNER, JERRELL H. *Nor Is It Over Yet: Florida in the Era of Reconstruction.* Gainesville: University Presses of Florida, 1974.

SIMKINS, FRANCIS B. *A History of the South.* 3d ed. New York: Alfred A. Knopf, 1963.

SIMMS, HENRY H. *Life of John Taylor.* Richmond: William Byrd Press, 1932.

STAMPP, KENNETH M. *The Peculiar Institution: Slavery in the Ante-Bellum South.* New York: Vintage Books, 1956.

UNGER, IRWIN. "The 'New Left' and American History: Some Recent Trends in United States Historiography." *American Historical Review* 72 (July 1967), 1237–43.

VIERECK, PETER. *Conservatism from John Adams to Churchill.* Princeton: D. Van Nostrand, 1956.

WALL, JOSEPH F. *Andrew Carnegie.* New York: Oxford University Press, 1970.

WEINBERG, ARTHUR, and WEINBERG, LILA. *The Muckrakers: The Era in Journalism that Moved America to Reform—The Most Significant Magazine Articles of 1902–1912.* New York: Simon and Schuster, 1961.

WELLBORN, CHARLES. *Twentieth Century Pilgrimage: Walter Lippman And The Public Philosophy.* Baton Rouge: Louisiana State University Press, 1969.

WHARTON, VERNON. "Reconstruction." In *Writing Southern History: Essays in Historiography in Honor of Fletcher Green*, pp. 295–315. Edited by Arthur S. Link and Rembert Patrick. Baton Rouge: Louisiana State University Press, 1967.

WILSON, EDMUND. *Patriotic Gore: Studies in the Literature of the American Civil War.* London: Andre Deutsch, 1962.

WOODWARD, C. VANN. *A History of the South.* Vol. 9. *Origins of the New South, 1877–1913.* Baton Rouge: Louisiana State University Press, 1951.

Index

This index includes: (1) principal writers and their works (abbreviated); (2) important general subjects; and (3) authors of secondary sources who have been quoted from and named in the text.

No attempt has been made to index the Notes and References and the Bibliography. However, important non-bibliographical information and statements have been indexed.

DATE DUE
